To my fellow collaborators,
Lothar Wolff, Paul Lammers, and Allan Sloane

Contents

Joy on Film

A film about Johann Sebastian Bach! For years it had been our dream. There was something about this man's music—its spirit, depth, delight, and joy—that compelled us to communicate its essence to a wide audience.

That dream of capturing joy on film has finally been realized with *The Joy of Bach*. Almost 25 years ago some seeds were planted for this project. Some of them germinated quickly. Others lay dormant, to sprout almost a generation later and finally to blossom joyously. For those of us permitted to husband this project, the satisfaction is enormous.

The first major feature film enterprise for Lutheran Film Associates had been a motion picture called *Martin Luther*. It was a remarkable success. What had begun as an audiovisual production by various Lutheran groups in the United States and Canada turned into a movie for the general public. Officials responsible for this production had been persuaded by the noted filmmaker Louis de Rochemont and his associates (principally Lothar

7

Wolff) that the story of Luther was as relevant to the human situation of the 1950s as it was to the 1520s.

When a film is a failure no one asks, "What next?" But when a movie is a success, everyone is eager to know whether it will be followed by another exciting project. Among the suggestions made was a film about Bach. Many considered the composer to be the most famous Lutheran of all time. It was felt that few people knew or appreciated the fact that he wrote much of his great music within and for the church and its worship. The story of Johann Sebastian Bach, like that of Luther, belongs not to one denominational family but to the world!

One man who particularly encouraged us to probe the possibilities of a film about Bach was the late Irving Pichel, Hollywood director and former actor, who had directed the Luther film for us. While in Minneapolis for the world premiere of *Martin Luther* he told me, "Bach must be your next film. It won't be easy. The biographical drama doesn't match the Reformation conflict in intensity. But the greatness is there. Not only is the Bach subject historically significant, it speaks to us in our need today." He added, "And the story belongs to you!"

There were others who prodded us also. Professor Hans Besch of Flensburg, Germany, was one. Besch had a vision of Bach and was as interested in having that vision captured on film as between the pages of a book. An authority on Bach's life and work, he emphasized the composer's contributions to both society and the church. He provided illustration after illustration of Bach's profound insight into the Christian gospel as revealed in his compositions. Professor Besch's enthusiasm helped to keep the dream of a Bach film alive.

Frequently in the 1950s and 1960s the trustees of Lu-

8

theran Film Associates would test, weigh, and earnestly consider the possibilities of following up the Luther film with one on the life of Bach. The idea was intriguing— but many hard questions had to be dealt with. Could the life story of Bach appeal to a general audience that might not know or care about the quality of his music? Could his music be presented in a popularized form without on the one hand compromising artistic integrity and on the other overtaxing an audience? Initial attempts to develop a script meeting these requirements were not successful. The LFA trustees remained confident that a film on Bach was in their future. But the search for the right approach and format would have to continue.

Among the factors that brought renewed consideration of a Bach film was the sheer explosion of interest in his music during the 1960s. The newspaper listings of Bach concerts within just the New York cultural scene seemed inexhaustible. Album releases of Bach works poured into the classical record shops in ever-greater numbers. *Time* magazine even devoted a cover story to Bach's growing popularity at Christmastime in 1968. The cover itself was a striking portrait by Ben Shahn over which *Time* had emblazoned Albert Schweitzer's slogan, "The Fifth Evangelist." The story described in rapturous terms what many have called the "Bach revolution":

Today, of course, Bach is universally ranked among the transcendent creators of Western civilization. Choral works that he turned out for rowdy schoolboys to sing in drafty provincial churches are cherished by the world's finest choruses. Keyboard exercises that he jotted down for his children and students still beguile and challenge great virtuosos. Instrumental pieces that he composed to curry favor with obscure princelings are judged among the glories of all chamber music.

The greatness of Bach has been recognized for more than a

century. But in all likelihood no age has better appreciated the true nature of his gifts.

. . . Even in the secularist atmosphere of the 20th century, his music rings with what Toronto Choral Conductor Elmer Iseler calls a positive, "D-major feeling about life." From the evidence of the 1968 holiday season, more and more listeners are trying to get into the same key (Dec. 27, 1968, p. 35).

In the early 1970s Lutheran Film Associates decided to take the Bach project off the back burner where it had been simmering for over a decade. A team of experts from the worlds of communications, music, and art was consulted, and was almost unanimous in its recommendation. The time had come to do a Bach film. If it had been done earlier it would have been ahead of its time. But now the time was ripe. And the essence of Bach (and the public excitement about him) is not to be found in the details of his biography. His life was not particularly colorful. What is exciting and dramatic and worthy of being communicated in a new way to film and television viewers throughout the world is Bach's *music*. If we tell the story of Bach's music and find a brilliant way to present that music on the screen we will have a hit!

Our consultants were convinced that we could carry out this task. With earlier films Lutheran Film Associates had demonstrated the ability to spend the time and money necessary to achieve quality with integrity. Bach should not be entrusted to the commercial producers and certainly not to Hollywood. We should do the film with the same loving care we bestowed on *Martin Luther*. This enthusiasm was, however, tempered with a warning. We should not expect that the entertainment industry will welcome a Bach film with open arms or even understand why we choose to offer it to them. We will have to show them. We should do the best job we can

11

◄ *Among other evidences of the popularity of Johann Sebastian Bach reflected in* The Joy of Bach *film is the Bach sweatshirt.*

with this opportunity, and take our chances in the competitive marketplace called show business.

We called on Lothar Wolff to help us. We could think of no more ideal producer. Not only had he already invested something of himself in us as producer of *Martin Luther* and in the earlier stages of the Bach project, but he had abundant international contacts and was accustomed to making films in Germany, France, England, Switzerland, and Italy as well as in the United States.

We also enlisted the cooperation of Paul Lammers, one of our LFA trustees who had been elected president of the corporation. As a Lutheran lay person Lammers had personal incentive to join in shaping up a film approach, and was also an active television director, specializing in daytime serial drama. He had worked at all three commercial TV networks.

Several other writers and film consultants were engaged to assist in the designing of the scenario. Howard Worth, who had directed a musical film about the Indian sitar player Ravi Shankar, brought proposals that helped us arrive at the final format. In over a year of collaboration he assisted us in focusing on the popularization of Bach's music.

Financing a major production is never a simple matter. The Bach project had its skeptics within our own board of trustees and among the leaders and officials who were to consider our request for subscriptions. Finally the American Lutheran Church and the Lutheran Church in America chose to participate, together contributing almost half of the budget. This financial support was matched by Lutheran Brotherhood, a fraternal insurance organization. After most of the filming had been completed, the George Gund Foundation of Cleveland made a grant to assist in the completion of the project.

12

It took many months to work out the funding, but once that was accomplished we were ready to translate our skeleton outline into a production plan. We needed a script, of course, but not the same kind normally used for filmmaking. More than a listing of scenes and dialog, we needed a cohesive assembly of viable musical and dramatic ideas—all linked by an appealing thematic thread. We needed more than a writer. We needed a creative team to stimulate, test, shape, and synthesize those musical and dramatic elements. But we did need a writer.

Lothar Wolff and I again turned to Allan Sloane, who had performed so effectively with the script responsibilities for *Question 7* and *Martin Luther*. His first prize-winning effort for Lutherans had been a landmark film about refugees in the late 1940s entitled *Answer for Anne*. In the 1950s Sloane had rejected the idea of a Bach film. He felt there was just not enough drama in Bach's biography to make a successful dramatic feature film. And he was right, of course. But we decided to approach him with this completely different idea—and he was immediately excited by it. He knew what we were striving for. His dedication to the goals of the project caused him to adapt his own busy schedule in order that the first steps of script development might begin right away.

All of us had favorites—favorite pieces from the repertoire of Bach's works and favorite performers we wanted to see in the film playing those selections. And we had favorite events from Bach's life that we hoped to weave into the show's fabric.

Sometimes we would spend our time together looking at a wall chart—full of pinned-up possibilities on multicolored cards—while listening to recordings of Bach's music. Someone would get an idea and sketch it out.

13

It would either be rejected out of hand or received tentatively and posted on the wall; sometimes we would applaud an idea jubilantly. Many of those we judged brilliant at first hearing were later dropped.

The process was slow, tedious, and often discouraging, but it was also stimulating and the source of much joy and excitement. Allan Sloane would fairly explode when a fresh idea hit him. But sometimes that idea would require toppling his carefully-crafted superstructure of scenes. Connections and linkages in this kind of show were important. Certain visual symbols, key words, or associational ideas were sought to carry viewers smoothly from one scene to the next. Sloane looked for contrapuntal ideas. He wanted the film to be layered with contrasts—then vs. now, conventional vs. unconventional, Europe vs. America, picture vs. soundtrack—and peppered with surprises.

Ultimately *The Joy of Bach* was to become a visual garland of performances by soloists and ensembles—instrumental and vocal—in a musical anthology of works from the creative soul of a single genius. But who would those performers be, and what music would be presented? The options in each case were many. Over the years we had amassed clippings, notes, and references about Bach performers that were both traditional and unconventional. Friends and associates who had learned of our project would tag items for us. Letters and phone calls would alert us to special opportunities. Library research would suddenly pay off when a single item among a packet of many collected listings would be exactly what we were looking for.

As a guide for selecting music and biographical incidents to include in the production we shaped a profile of Johann Sebastian Bach that reflected some of the more dramatic moments in his career—his being jailed, for example, and his being honored by Frederick the Great —while at the same time indicating that he was an organ expert, keyboard virtuoso, composer, court musician, and church musician. The film would have to have choral music, chamber music, organ and harpsichord works, instrumental solos, and concertos, and within these categories certain compositions would simply have to be included.

The process by which we sought to capture the joy of Bach on film did not have the kind of orderly, textbook precision we might have originally expected. It couldn't be a linear production development from concept to treatment to funding to scripting to preproduction planning to filming to editing to release. Instead we had to catch opportunities when and as they occurred. If we were to get performances on film from busy artists we would have to accommodate their schedules by going to them. Of course there were problems. There always are in any large filming project. One of our major problems was the mobility factor; there were dozens of locations in at least five countries.

One potential problem we thought might develop didn't. We had hoped to film in "Bach country," at or near the actual sites where Bach lived and worked. That meant working in the German Democratic Republic (East Germany), and we were concerned about the possibility of special permissions and restrictions. All of this was simplified when we were able to hire crews and production personnel directly from the state-operated television organization. Instead of anxiety, obfuscation, and delay, we were rewarded with gracious accommodation, efficient expediting of logistics, top professionalism of technicians and artists, and a congenial spirit among

15

all assigned to our team. They knew why we were there. Bach was a part of their lives, part of their national heritage. They were genuinely pleased to be working with Americans, helping us to find and capture on film the joy of Bach.

Behind the flowing melodies and colorful settings shown on the screen there are moments that to us are especially worth remembering:

● There was much consternation when the musicians engaged to play in Bach's orchestra showed up for the filming at the castle representing the Coethen court. One was a woman and three of the men had beards. Baroque orchestras did not have women or bearded men! The session was almost cancelled but at the last minute the problem was solved: the woman musician dressed up in a man's clothing, one player was paid extra to shave off his beard, the music was recorded in advance by the full ensemble, and during the shooting stand-ins took the place of the two violinists who were unable to lose their bearded identity (they couldn't risk looking different from their passport photos).

● The frustration of finding a place for the camera and lights in a room full of mirrors—in the historic *Neue Palais* in Potsdam, in a music room containing Frederick the Great's piano and flute—was exacerbated by the curator's stopping the shooting every 10 or 15 minutes, when the heat from the lights rose to a point beyond which the priceless paintings might be damaged.

● After lugging heavy equipment to the top of one of the foothills near Big Sky, Montana, cameraman Ray Christensen discovered that a lens box he needed had been left in a stationwagon on the road far below. The "star" insisted that he run down to retrieve it. He was

16

Members of the Brooklyn Boys' Chorus, ▶
conducted by James McCarthy, enjoy
singing "Jesu, Joy of Man's Desiring."

Christopher Parkening, the concert guitarist. He said he felt at home in those mountains and wanted the exercise. When the camera was finally rolling, Parkening calmly played the gentle, "Sheep May Safely Graze," with no hint of breathlessness.

● Some performers were relaxed about their work in front of the camera and others were fussy. Undoubtedly the most fastidious was Rosalyn Tureck, who had to be assured that her playing of the Gigue from the Third English Suite not only looked right but sounded right. It was a complicated setup, with Madame Tureck starting the performance on a tiny clavichord, moving to her harpsichord, continuing on her piano, and completing the piece on the electronic keyboard of the Polymoog synthesizer. There were 23 takes before she was completely satisfied. She also insisted on being in the studio when the soundtracks from these four separately filmed performances were joined; she instructed the engineer when to add or remove "highs" and "lows." But we didn't object a bit—for us it meant that Bach's music for our production was getting the tender, loving care it deserved. And we better understood the nature of artistry.

The fun and excitement and pleasure of a production are important mostly for those who have shared in it. But they become significant if they are are somehow ultimately reflected back from the screen. Others will have to judge that. But I wonder if the spirit of a production, especially as it is subtlely communicated through performance, doesn't color and shade music. Can more joy be communicated by performers who are themselves captured by their music? When I look at the faces of the Brooklyn Boys Chorus, radiating sheer delight in singing Bach, I know the answer!

18

1

Joy in Performing Bach

"The one composer I most adore playing is Bach because everything he wrote he seemed to write for the mouth organ!"

Larry Adler was speaking. At a Greenwich Village coffeehouse he had been standing for almost an hour performing Mozart, Debussy, Bartok, Rachmaninoff, and Gershwin to the delight of the patrons who had crowded in. The sound of his tiny instrument amazed and excited the listeners. The mouth organ (he doesn't use the term *harmonica*) was ideal for that intimate setting. But even in a large concert hall he had enthralled his audiences with his virtuosity as a soloist with major symphony orchestras. He chose Bach to climax his coffeehouse show. It was the same lovely Siciliano he performs in *The Joy of Bach.*

For those who play his music there is a magic and a magnetism about Johann Sebastian Bach. It is difficult to put into words. A musician comes to sense it as a special experience quite apart from the pleasure of simply hear-

ing the music played by someone else. One may really understand this only on discovering that there is joy in the very process of reading the notes Bach once wrote down and of recreating the sounds he himself heard. It is a spiritual thing, linking composer with performer in a musical communion.

This is what makes film director George Roy Hill play a little Bach on the piano every day. It's also what makes a street musician in New York decide to play only Bach on his little electric keyboard strapped to a shopping cart, which he wheels into doorways near busy intersections. "I tried Haydn and Mozart," he says. But they can't be "played in the streets" like Bach can. Bach "reminds people of their nature."

It is this same mystical and spiritual quality that motivated the great cellist and conductor, Pablo Casals, to play Bach each morning.

For the past eighty years I have started each day in the same manner. It is not a mechanical routine but essential to my daily life. I go to the piano and I play two preludes and fugues of Bach. I cannot think of doing otherwise. It is a sort of benediction on the house. But that is not its only meaning for me. It is a rediscovery of the world of which I have the joy of being a part. It fills me with awareness of the wonder of life, with a feeling of the incredible marvel of being a human being. The music is never the same for me, never. Each day it is something new, fantastic and unbelievable. That is Bach—like nature, a miracle! (*Joys and Sorrows*, Simon and Schuster, 1970, p. 17)

This is the same Casals who, according to legend, when asked what he would say if he could talk to all the people in the world, responded, "I would say, 'Do you like war?' I am sure that all those millions of people would say 'No.' And then I would play a Bach piece for them."

Another musical pioneer who, like Casals, was cham-

21

◀ *Larry Adler captivates a group of children with his skilled performance of Bach's music on the traditional instrument he calls a "mouth organ."*

pioning Johann Sebastian Bach years before it was popular to do so was the late Wanda Landowska. Her harpsichord recordings of the great keyboard literature helped many music lovers discover Bach and begin a love affair with him. The joy she also felt from playing Bach was something spiritual:

Everything is close to Bach, and everything in Bach's music is close to us, is part of our own life of misery, despair, or bliss. Bach never climbs on a pedestal to preach or admonish. . . . Why does a melodic line, as beautiful as it may be, even a melodic phrase of Chopin, for instance, become tiresome while the melodic line of Bach can withstand more severe tests? Because there is something eternal in Bach's music, something that makes us wish to hear again what has just been played. This renewal gives us a glimpse of eternity (*Landowska on Music*, Stein and Day, 1964, pp. 234-235).

Perhaps no one did more to introduce Bach to mass audiences than Leopold Stokowski. His recordings, beginning in the 1930s, became very popular. He had a gift of transcribing Bach's chorale preludes for symphony orchestra. He brought to this task (especially when he was conductor of the Philadelphia Orchestra) a romanticism that proved to be soft, soothing, and luxuriously appealing to people hungry for those restorative and reassuring sounds. His somewhat sentimental treatment of Bach was repudiated by purists, who hastened to point out that the music—in order to be more faithful to the leaner and cleaner Baroque timbre—deserved a more austere adaptation. But Stokowski, who began his musical career in America as an organist playing Bach, understood his audience. And he understood the composer, too:

In the character of the man who so revolutionized the music of his own time and so influenced that of centuries to come was a remarkable balance between the heart, head and hand. From his heart came the intensity of expression and from his head came his superb mastery of counterpoint, fugue and every other form of polyphonic music. His dexterity of hand amazed all of those of his contemporaries who were capable of understanding his technical mastery (*New York Times Magazine,* July 23, 1950, p. 17).

A remarkable communication breakthrough in the effort by Leopold Stokowski to popularize the music of Bach came with the maestro's collaboration on film with Mickey Mouse. Walt Disney created the movie *Fantasia* that innovatively brought the music of various composers to the screen. In that film Stokowski conducted the Toccata and Fugue in D Minor and helped millions discover some exciting new sounds from an old composer.

Virgil Fox is one popular performer who has caught joy in the playing of Bach's music. He communicates its dynamism to vast audiences (especially youthful audiences) through his "Heavy Organ" touring performances, which include David Snyder's light show called "Revelation Lights." An excerpt from it is included in *The Joy of Bach* film, complete with the rhythmic clapping of hands to the tempo of Bach's *Fugue ala' Gigue.*

In the *New York Times* Richard Dyer described the amazing phenomenon of a Virgil Fox concert:

He sways his torso and swings his hands aloft and makes a great show of changing the stops cross-handed. A spotlight on those pumps makes sure you don't forget he's moving down there, too. The swell pedal, that aural zoom lens, brings the music forward and takes it away, and the playing is alternately and in various combinations very soft and very loud and very fast and very slow. The registrations may be gaudy, the pedal on Fox's Rodgers Tour Organ may honk away while the upper divisions, blowsily amplified, sometimes sound like the ultimate accordion, but no one can deny that Fox hits a powerful lot of notes, almost all of them the right ones.

Fox's face, sometimes tossed back, sometimes turned to the crowd, telegraphs the looming effect and tells you what to think. His assistant, David Snyder, hovering over the "Revelation Lights" console in a Flash Gordon outfit, rinses Fox green and blue "to enunciate, to further describe what I feel are the intentions of the composer and the style of Virgil Fox." The play of lights on the giant screen suggests that some kind of cosmic popcorn popper is at work; a figure shaped like a tooth does a little gigue; at the end amid flashing jukebox colors and cumulo-nimbus clouds a big Bach medallion emerges from the center, floating serenely among astral events just like the globe in the credits for Universal-International Pictures" (Sept. 9, 1974, p. D19).

Michael Steinberg, writing in the *Boston Globe,* dismissed the "spermy" light show and characterized Fox's operation as a "mixture of showmanship, Bach, lights, slightly tattered virtuosity, homoerotic fantasies, animadversions on religion (pro) and drugs (contra)." But in reporting this in the *Times,* Dyer also noted that a teenager at one of Fox's Pennsylvania concerts turned to him to say, "I never thought I would enjoy Bach."

Virgil Fox enjoys Bach. He says, "All we have to do is open up our pores and let him in. . . . He felt everything and because he did he has a message for all of us."

The joy of performing Bach for the sake of the doers rather than the hearers applies to singers as well as instrumentalists. The Princeton Society of Musical Amateurs in New Jersey schedules a half dozen sing-ins each season and one or two Bach works are always included. People in the community— professors, students, homemakers, business people, teachers—come together to read through the *Christmas Oratorio* or the *St. John Passion.* A professional orchestra accompanies the chorus. Professional soloists are included and a well-known conductor is engaged from Princeton University or the Westminster Choir College. Each amateur singer pays a fee for the privilege. All the elements of a concert are collected except an audience.

The idea of "Bach for the fun of it" has been picked up elsewhere, as this item in the *New York Times* shows:

It was a grand night for singing Tuesday evening, when more than 300 people from all walks of life converged on New York University's Loeb Student Center to sing Bach's Mass in B Minor, simply for the joy of doing it. The program was the last in a series of six public "summer sings" sponsored by N.Y.U., and directed by David Randolph, conductor and commentator.

Bearded, baldish or bewigged, and attired in everything from basic black with pearls to mid-thigh, cut-off jeans, the singers lined up to pay a $1.50 fee and to pick up their scores.

"The Bach B Minor always brings them out," someone said in the crush (July 28, 1966, p. 24).

The music of Johann Sebastian Bach gives joy to those who play it, in part because it seduces the emotional side of the brain with grace and loveliness while at the same time winning the intellectual side with an orderliness of almost mathematical precision. The playing of a Bach fugue, for example, can be fun to work through just as solving a puzzle can be both relaxing and mentally challenging at the same time. The two kinds of experiences are held in a musically marvelous tension.

Yehudi Menuhin understands this. He has said that Bach is "characteristic of our era in that his music is equally balanced between mathematics and emotion." The famous violinist demonstrated this point for *The Joy of Bach* when he allowed cameras to film him at his home at Highgate near London playing "Tempo di Bourree" from Partita 1 in B Minor for Unaccompanied Violin. He had only one day at home between his arrival from Greece and his departure for Moscow, but he neverthe-

less made himself available for the film project because he wanted so much to have world television audiences understand the kinship musicians like himself felt for Bach.

"A crystalline logic underlies all of Bach's work," Menuhin has said, "which is one reason why he is so often the favorite composer of mathematicians and scientists. But his music also throbs with a living pulse; his rhythms and harmonic modulations, however controlled, evolve with seeming spontaneity. His endlessly inventive melodies, however neatly they fit into a scheme, rise and fall and intertwine with a lyrical life of their own. The most solid of his constructions are nevertheless charged with energy and intensity" (*Time*, Dec. 27, 1968, pp. 36-37).

Rosalyn Tureck has devoted over 40 years to her pilgrimage in search of the secrets of Bach. She, perhaps more than most other performers and musicologists, has discovered many of his mysteries. She has penetrated deeply into the music—immersing herself, so to speak, inside his compositions—so she can not only concertize with his music but also write and teach and explain his genius.

The accoutrements of Bach surround Madame Tureck in her apartment in Manhattan—the complete library of his works in the Bach Gesellschaft edition, a marble bust of the composer, a portrait, an autographed picture of Albert Schweitzer, and of course her precious instruments: clavichord, harpsichord, piano, and even an electronic synthesizer.

Her editions of some of Bach's keyboard music, the *Chromatic Fantasia and Fugue* and the *Italian Concerto*, particularly, are recognized as landmarks of Bach scholarship. To spread the gospel of a living Bach, Rosalyn

27

◀ *After moving from the clavichord to the harpsichord to the piano, Rosalyn Tureck concludes one of Bach's gigues on an electronic synthesizer.*

Tureck established and founded the International Bach Society. Lectures, concerts, demonstrations, master classes, discussions, publications, tapes—these are all part of the educational program she instituted almost single-handedly.

Tureck started her musical training at age 10 and even then was fascinated by Bach's works. But her conversion to a dedicated discipleship came at 17. She told the story to Allan Kozinn:

> It was on a Wednesday in December, just before my 17th birthday. I started the A minor Prelude and Fugue in Book I (Well-Tempered Clavier), and just as I started the fugue, I lost consciousness. Totally. I don't know if it was for five minutes or half an hour. I only know that when I came to, I knew everything I had to do. I had a new insight into the structure of Bach, and even more profoundly, into the concept behind that structure—the whole psychological concept of form and the architecture that this form gives rise to.
>
> I knew I could never again play the piano the way I had been taught, and that I had to create a different technique. These realizations were simultaneous. I get a chill even as I talk about it (*New York Times*, Oct. 9, 1977, p. D38).

"One of the reasons Bach is so fascinating to me is that he is so difficult," Tureck told us. "Even though I have spent so much of my life playing Bach and thinking about his music, he still remains difficult. And this is for me the joy." She laughed, "It's not masochism! Although I love all other kinds of music, I have found that in Bach I never, never become bored. I have never tired of it. When I repeat Bach over and over there is never a weariness. It's always fresh. I'm always finding new things."

Madame Tureck, who has lived and concertized in England as well as in the U.S., revealed that the Queen Mother also appreciates Bach's music. She once said, "You know, Bach has something for everybody." Tureck added that it brings joy to those "who know nothing about music as well as to those who know everything. The simplicity is so profound."

For Rosalyn Tureck, Bach is "a universal mind and a universal soul. And for that reason I don't play him only on instruments of that period." She was already experimenting with electronic music in the 1930s, and once demonstrated the theremin (the earliest of all electronic instruments) at a concert. She has been a consultant to the Moog company, and has spent hours developing different and distinctive sounds on synthesizer keyboards in order to realize new audio dimensions for her beloved Bach.

Christopher Parkening, who includes Bach in his guitar concerts and has recorded an album of exclusively Bach works, got "hooked" on Bach from listening to Andres Segovia play the Courante from the Third Cello Suite. Parkening says he listened to the recording over and over again, and it changed his life. He was able to study with Segovia and came to perceive and appreciate that great artist's brotherhood with Bach.

For his performance of "Sheep May Safely Graze" in *The Joy of Bach*, Parkening suggested that filming take place near his ranch in Bozeman, Montana. It was springtime, and the snow was still lingering on the peaks of the mountains along the Gallatin Canyon. He agreed to the difficult task of performing the work over and over again during a full day's shooting that involved 10 different camera locations.

Parkening told us that for that particular piece he had to develop a new technique which he had never seen used before. It first involved a very unusual tuning of the bass string to a low C, and the fifth string to a low G. "There were left-handed fingerings in the piece which I had never done before. I could say that a special left-hand technique was invented to play the piece. We had to name it when we published the music and we called it a 'double bar.' Without going into it fully, I can describe it as a complicated bar chord over two frets simultaneously. It was kind of difficult to do and certainly a challenge."

Parkening says that, depending upon his mood, he often prefers Bach to anything else. "I don't know if I can say why. It's simple but complicated, beautiful but profound." He said that because it is possible to play both the melody and the accompaniment together on the guitar, Bach can be played without needing another instrument. "You have so many different colors on the instrument—there are five middle Cs on the guitar, all of which have a different color. Bach transcribes for the guitar beautifully."

When pianist Clara Schumann hurt her right hand in 1877 and couldn't play, her good friend Johannes Brahms sent her a gift, an arrangement he had made of Bach's *Chaconne* (for violin) for the piano to be played with the left hand only. He wrote:

The *Chaconne* is, in my opinion, one of the most wonderful and most incomprehensible pieces of music. Using the technique adapted to a small instrument, the man writes a whole world of the deepest thoughts and most powerful feelings. If I could picture myself writing, or even conceiving, such a piece I am sure that the extreme excitement and emotional tension would have driven me mad.

If one has no supremely great violinist at hand, the most exquisite of joys is probably simply to let the Chaconne ring in one's mind. But the piece certainly inspires one to occupy one's self with it somehow. One does not always want to hear music actually played, and in any case Joachim is not always there, so one tries it otherwise. But whether I try it with an orchestra or piano, the pleasure is always spoiled for me.

There is only one way in which I can secure undiluted joy

30

Flutist Jean-Pierre Rampal performs one ▶
of Bach's compositions for unaccompanied
flute from atop the Centre Georges
Pompidou in Paris.

from the piece, though on a small and only approximate scale, and that is when I play it with the left hand alone. . . . If it does not exert you too much—which is what I am afraid of— you ought to get great fun out of it (*Composers on Music*, Pantheon, 1956, pp. 211-212).

When asked by the *Washington Star* how she would explain Bach to someone who knows nothing about him, the founder and president of the Johann Sebastian Bach International Piano Competitions, teacher and pianist Raissa Tselentis, said "You don't explain, really, great music to anybody. You expose them to it, and before you expose them to it you throw out a few guidelines, tell them what to listen for."

She said that the first thing she tells her students to listen for are the songs. "In Bach you have a melody against melody, a song that sings at the same time as the other song sings. They both have their own identities and character. That is what we call polyphonic. . . . There are people who are so sensitive, whose souls are so at- tuned to beauty that, though they are not really musically educated, they have affinity for beauty wherever they hear it or see it. These people always immediately re- spond to Bach" (*Washington Star*, Nov. 26, 1976, p. 1).

To any musician of letters, there is the definite snob appeal of reveling in Bach's web of melody, fugue themes, inversions, retrogrades, augmentations, diminutions, and other examples of schematic jargon. So writes Howard Klein:

But I always find myself getting lost in the emotional warmth. The brain suddenly loses its clarity, the eyes film over, the faraway look enters, and I'm hooked. I could as well be watching "Hamlet" as listening to "The Art of the Fugue." How was it possible to make so dramatic an experience of fugal exercises—what, to counterpoint teachers, is the Rosetta

Stone of their exacting discipline? Oh, Bach, I hope you knew how great you were (*New York Times,* July 13, 1969, sect. 2, p. 24).

Bach knew he had a great gift. And he wanted his music to be enjoyed. The dedications he wrote on some of the flyleaf pages of his manuscripts testify to that. "For the use and profit of the musical youth desirous of learning as well as for the pastime of those already skilled in this study . . ." *(Well-Tempered Clavier).* "Upright instruction wherein the lovers of the clavier, and especially those desirous of learning, are shown in a clear way. . . . not alone to have good *inventions* (ideas), but to develop the same well, and above all to arrive at a singing style in playing . . ." *(Inventions).* "Keyboard practice consisting in preludes, allemandes, courantes, sarabandes, gigues, minuets, and other galanteries composed for music lovers, to refresh their spirits . . ." *(Clavier Übung).*

The parade of testimonials from Bach lovers who have discovered joy in the playing of Bach's music is just beginning. The parade includes novices who may only have arduously worked out the notes and fingerings for the two simple melodies of an Anna Magdalena Notebook minuet as the left hand and right hand play tag with one another. And it includes the celebrated concert artists who have probed into the depths of Bach's work.

To all of us who hum or strum, who sing or swing, who blow or bow, who use our hands or play in bands, Johann Sebastian Bach offers for any mood and any season the gift of joy!

2

Joy in
Dancing to Bach

From his harpsichord Johann Sebastian Bach looked out approvingly at the two young couples dancing his minuet. They were elegantly dressed, blending nicely with the gilded mirrors, the sparkling crystal chandeliers, the polished parquet floors, and the walls covered with landscapes and portraits. Bach could see beyond the dancers to the bewigged gentlemen and satined ladies gossiping and laughing but not really listening to his music or admiring the grace of the dancers.

At the Coethen court of Prince Leopold it was Bach's job to entertain, and he had been a professional musician long enough to accept the functionalism of his art. It was perhaps reward enough for him that the dancers loved dancing to the music that he had composed and was now playing with his little orchestra.

Bach knew about the art of dance. When he was a teenager in the choir school at Lüneburg he was chosen as accompanist for the *Mettenchor* after his voice changed and he could no longer sing soprano. Because there was

34

also a dance department at that school, with a dance master in charge, it is very likely that Bach was also co-opted for accompanying the dance lessons. If so, he had firsthand training in the various forms of courtly dance: allemande, courante, sarabande, passepied, gavotte, and gigue, together with the minuet and other specialized dances. At Coethen he incorporated his knowledge into composing various suites that were collections of dances. He had also likely learned about the French influence on dance, as well as on music, when he visited the French-patterned court at Celle during his student days.

In order to make the court dance sequence in *The Joy of Bach* film as authentic as possible, one of the top experts in Baroque dance of the German Democratic Republic was enlisted as choreographer. Manfred Schnelle, himself a dancer and teacher at the Technical School for the Art of Dance in Leipzig, explained that for most of the courtiers in Bach's time dancing was a spectator sport. Hardly ever would there be more than one or two couples dancing. While all young persons among the nobility would have training in dance, the rules for each type of dance were rather formidable; the ladies and gentlemen visiting the castle would be reluctant to dance in public unless they had trained and practiced. Therefore the youth would be asked to dance while the others watched or talked among themselves.

Herr Schnelle had spent many months training the two couples from the Leipzig dance school in the nuances of the minuet that was danced to the music from Bach's fourth orchestral suite. He had presented these same students in a recital of music and dance from the Baroque period at Karl Marx University in Leipzig, and had also participated in a re-creation of dance from the Bach era staged in Leipzig's ornate Hanseatic Old City Hall.

Schnelle also does modern dance, and like so many of his counterparts in western Europe and America, he has used Bach's music for his contemporary expression. In 1964 he interpreted the choreography of Marianne Vogelsang in a dance called "Poetry, Language of the World," based on the Prelude in E Minor of Book I of Bach's *Well-Tempered Clavier.*

There is something innately spirited in Bach's music that makes it ideal to dance to. It's the rhythm, of course, but it's more than that. In the dance collection of the Performing Arts Research Center of the New York Public Library there is a list of 112 different dances that have been choreographed to Bach's music. The list includes the great figures of both ballet and modern dance—Humphrey, Bejart, Limon, Shawn Weidman, Balanchine, Robbins, Taylor, Lubovitch, and more.

Concerto Barocco, one of the first classical ballets to use Bach's music, was choreographed by George Balanchine in 1940. Critic Edwin Denby called it "the masterpiece of a master choreographer." He said, "It has only eleven dancers; it is merely straight dancing to music— no sex story, no period angle, no violence. . . . It has a power of rhythm and flow; in a wealth of figuration it is everywhere transparent, fresh, graceful and noble" (*Looking at Dance,* Popular Library, 1968, p. 117).

Balanchine used the music of Bach's Concerto in D Minor for Two Violins. About it he said, "Bach's great concerto can stand alone. Some people then wonder, why arrange a ballet to such music? Why not arrange ballets to music that is more dependent, music that dancing can 'fill out'? The answer is that bad music often inspires bad dancing, bad choreography. . . . Bach had

36

In the plaza of the Centre Pompidou, ▶
Andre Benichou and his Well-Tempered
Three perform the Gavotte from English
Suite 6 in D Minor.

no idea of composing music for a ballet; but in listening to this music, it is possible to conceive of movement that harmonizes with the score. Actually, it seems to me that the music of Bach and Mozart is always very close to dancing. It would be wrong to say that all music should be danced, but I think the greatest music is never far from dancing. I agree with the poet who said that music rots when it is too far removed from the dance, just as poetry rots when it departs too far from music" (*Balanchine's Complete Stories of Great Ballets*, Doubleday, 1977, pp. 125, 779).

Jerome Robbins introduced his choreography to Bach's *Goldberg Variations* at the New York State Theater in 1971, and this too became an immediate hit. As a pianist plays the theme and 30 variations from a platform to the left of the proscenium arch, the ensemble, soloists, and couples in 18th century costumes delight the audience with the many moods of Bach. The piece was written for Bach's pupil, Johann Theophilus Goldberg. He had been hired to entertain Count von Kayserling, Russian ambassador to the Dresden Court, who suffered from insomnia. Neither the music nor the ballet is calculated to put anyone to sleep!

In 1972 Balanchine produced another ballet to Bach's music, but this one employed a score that had been arranged by Igor Stravinsky. He wrote *Choral Variations on Bach's "Vom Himmel Hoch."*

The use of Bach's music in modern dance—as distinguished from ballet—was pioneered by the late Doris Humphrey, who for years collaborated with Charles Weidman (she died in 1958). Her most famous dance set to Bach's music was *Passacaglia and Fugue in C Minor,* intended to reflect humanity's "dogged reiteration of faith." For Jose Limon she created a dance to Bach's violin *Chaconne.* She has also used the familiar "Air on the G String" (from Orchestral Suite 3) and Partita in G Major.

Critics have acclaimed *Esplanade* by the Paul Taylor Dance Company as one of the great modern dance works thus far produced. Choreographer Taylor took one movement from Bach's Violin Concerto in E and two additional movements from the Concerto for Two Violins in D Minor (also used in *Concerto Barocco*) and has his dancers run, walk, tumble, and leap energetically. This dance was shown nationally over PBS television as a part of the Dance in America series.

Another television transmission of a dance to Bach's music was *And Joy Is My Witness,* danced by Pearl Lang and Bruce Marks first in "Omnibus" over CBS in 1957 and later on "Frontiers of Faith" over NBC in 1960. Ms. Lang used Bach's Toccata for Organ in C Major.

Why do dancers like to use the music of Johann Sebastian Bach for their creative constructs and performances? Jeff Duncan of the University of Maryland, Baltimore County (who choreographed the modern dance in *The Joy of Bach* film to the Presto from the Fifth Harpsichord Concerto for the Jeff Duncan Dancers) says that Bach gives such a "kinetic feeling."

"Part of the joy is in the energy generated by the way Bach composes," Duncan told us as we were filming in the new performing arts center on his campus. He explained "kinetic feeling" as a term that comes from kinesiology, "a study of muscles and how they act and react and align." He said that a dancer seems to have "an extra awareness of the connection of the sensibilities to the muscles that make movements. We sense our environment by our muscles and it motivates those sensitivities in a very strong way."

Duncan thought that Bach's music was popular for dance, first of all, because of its full sound. "The sound is so satisfying in a harmonic sense, especially the big juicy works like the *concerti*. They give you such a full sound to dance against, coupled with a supreme, clear structure. This helps choreographers with their own structure. Couple this strong structure with the luscious harmonic sound and it really lifts you." He also explained how this relates to dance interpretation. "Dance is very nebulous. In other words, how does one make a dance? There is nothing you write down. How do you recapture movement? Part of the effort in bringing together the art and method or craft of choreography in the last decade or so has been to take the musical structure somewhat as the model. Although dance has its own particular kind of structure, the musician and the dancer have the same kind of breath movement. There are two basic kinds of phrasing: breath phrasing and metric phrasing. With Bach you have them both."

Other Baroque composers, Duncan hastened to add, have some of this quality also. He felt that the dance forms that they used in their suites were closely allied with the actual dances seen in the courts of that period. "Also, what is nice is that Bach had wonderfully different moods." Especially in the counterpoint and in the fugues, "it's a mathematical thing, but even so, it still has this incredible life pulse behind it."

Duncan said that when he worked out the modern dance routine for *The Joy of Bach* he first immersed himself in the music completely in order to absorb its mood, rhythm, and structure. "Then I would step away and improvise without music to get certain rhythms worked out for myself. I didn't want to duplicate anything or 'Mickey Mouse' it, as we call it. And so I would build what I felt

41

◀ *The Swingle Singers, a concert and recording ensemble, perform Bach's "Little" Organ Fugue with a jazz beat.*

was a valid dance structure against his music, connecting at certain moments. It was almost like two things going together to make a third thing. I improvised solely from the music's kinetic impulse, discovering movement, phrases and motifs that I felt were appropriate to the music and yet had a validity in their own right." He said that he didn't want his dance to make the same statement as the music. "It's almost a visual counterpoint to the musical statement."

For many people, one of the most surprising dances in *The Joy of Bach* is the flamenco dance. A researcher exploring dance possibilities noticed that the summer program at Jacob's Pillow, a workshop and festival near Lee, Massachusetts, included a Bach number being danced by the flamenco dancer Teodoro Morca. The producers were understandably skeptical. But the very oddity of it was persuasive enough to have it checked out.

Seeing Morca dance to Bach's Toccata and Fugue in D Minor was electrifying! The drama and visual excitement of it left no doubt but that it must be filmed immediately, whether it would ultimately be incorporated into the final film or not. It was the first filming done for *The Joy of Bach*, and all of those who saw the rushes agreed that it epitomized the motifs of delight, surprise, and variety that the production was aiming at.

The music was written for organ and is one of the best known of all Bach's compositions. Morca danced to a recorded performance by organist E. Power Biggs, but selected rather a pedal harpsichord version. The script for *The Joy of Bach* already called for the Toccata to be used as the demonstration piece Bach himself would play in a reconstructed vignette. The hope was that the historical, traditional pipe organ rendition would be counterpointed by following it with the flamboyant flamenco.

42

The synthesis worked. The only problem was that the sound, recorded on location at Jacob's Pillow, was not as good as it needed to be. The rapid-fire click of castanets and staccato foot tapping had to be picked up on a microphone and mixed with the prerecorded sound of the late E. Power Biggs from his recording. It was decided to overdub or rerecord the sound, and months after the original filming Teodoro Morca came to New York to recreate his dance in a studio in front of a movie screen. There he danced alone for the benefit of microphones and recording machines, listening on headphones as he watched himself on the screen, perfectly resynchronizing each click and clack of castanet and each whirring tap and stomp of his feet.

During this postproduction dubbing he talked about his discovery that Bach was ideal music for a flamenco dancer: "It changed my whole life." He explained that he had been introduced to Bach by his wife Isabel, also a dancer in the Spanish style. When Isabel and Teo were married they had a Bach concert as a part of their wedding. "The more I heard of Bach the more I realized how universal he was," Morca said, "and one day I bought a record of E. Power Biggs playing the pedal harpsichord. It was so emotional, and I immediately related it to the flamenco, to the emotion that people feel in flamenco. I started to move to it. I then set it aside because it seemed so out of the mold of Spanish classical dance. But when I was rehearsing it, a friend of mine, a very fine dancer, was watching. He went away on tour and came back in about two months, and the very first thing he said to me was, 'Whatever happened to that dance you were doing to Bach?' The very fact he remembered it said to me that it must have been interesting, so I pursued it, choreographed it, and, as I said, it changed me because it made me move a whole other way. It opened up a lot of channels of movement."

After seeing the new dance, another dance friend commented, "I never realized that Bach was so dramatic and sensual and flowing!" Morca added that "this was what I felt myself without my explaining what my concept was. So it was a very exciting thing when I finally got it choreographed and started to dance to it. Of course it was accepted and, needless to say, I use it in my repertoire quite a bit because it does cause a very excited reaction that is ninety-nine percent favorable."

Is Bach different for a dancer from Vivaldi or other Baroque composers? "Yes. He has what in Spain is called *duende*—he has a lot of soul—not that Vivaldi doesn't. But Bach is just very emotional and dramatic to me. Plus the fact that Bach is very flamenco to me because I can improvise within the structure of Bach. I think he would like that. He was a great improviser."

This was surprising to hear, because on the screen it seems that Morca's dancing was not improvised at all. It seems highly disciplined, highly structured, and very exciting. "That's the point I would like to get across to the audience. However, when I dance it, I will for instance many times start a pattern on the left foot one time and the right foot the other time. I might come in one bar ahead or one bar late. It doesn't change the thing at all. There is a certain flexible freedom. Flamenco is that way—an improvised form within a structure. There might be a rhythm of 12, and I can do anything I want as long as I don't go out of that 12 pattern. It's like saying you can do anything you want in this room but you can't go out. In the fugue the structure of that fugue gives me that freedom. I know where it's going.

"I don't think there is a choreographer that doesn't use

44

Bach," the flamenco dancer asserted. "I think they hear first the rhythm. If you hear a basic rhythm you get involved. Your body moves in rhythm and you start to listen that way. An experienced choreographer wants to get past the rhythm. I think they all feel the same thing —the universality. He has a universal air about his music that is elusive to explain. In Spanish it's called *aire*. It's an air. Like when someone walks in a room and people say 'He has a lot of class.' They don't just mean the clothes. Maybe it's the way he carries himself. It makes you say, 'I'd like to meet that person.' He exudes class or style or whatever. Well, Bach's music has that air about it. You feel if you could dance to it you would just float over the footlights because it's so beautiful."

Isabel Morca has choreographed what her husband calls a "gorgeous" first movement to Bach's Third Brandenburg Concerto. It has a blend of East Indian and Spanish. He dances the second movement. He has also completed a new dance to another unlikely Bach work, the Chromatic Fantasy and Fugue. "I don't think it has ever been choreographed and I thought I was very presumptuous to attack it. But I still feel about it like I did about the Toccata and Fugue in D Minor. And it's working."

Teodoro Morca in talking about dancing to Bach's music mentioned that it had a sensual quality. Does this refer to the rhythm or to the whole thing? "To all of it. When you are dancing—and of course the human body is the dancer's instrument—you have a tendency to flow. I mean it in a very flowing and beautiful way. It's not a sexual type of sensuality. You noticed perhaps the part in the film where I just kind of run around the stage and lift one leg and stretch and stretch and then . . . Boom! Hit the floor. That pulling is what it is. Even though

there's a definite beat, you might be almost standing still. Like a beginning of a walk, like a cat—that's sensual—like a tiger stalking. It is probably the hardest thing to teach in dance."

Morca said that he found it very exciting to dance in *The Joy of Bach* because it seemed to justify all the things he had been saying about the universality of Bach and the adaptability of Bach's music to all sorts of forms of expression. "Here I am dancing in a film that has all these different things in it. Obviously the thought patterns are out there in the spheres—people thinking like we are thinking. I think there is more Bach interest now than ever before. What it's saying is that here is a universal source of inspiration that is as timeless today as ever and it's to be appreciated. I think people are very ready!"

As a foundation or platform for dance of various sorts this is perhaps just beginning for the music of Johann Sebastian Bach. As we discover on the screen in the film, Bach is ideal for the stately and genteel court dances of the 18th century, serves the purpose of ballet and modern dance choreographers, and can even be adapted for the classical Spanish school of dancing that includes flamenco. More than that, Bach's music slides easily into a jazz beat or a rock beat. And for disco dance music, it can readily be arranged, as the Dutch disco group Ekseption has demonstrated with their version of *Vivace* based on the Violin Concerto in A Minor.

In the famed Brooklyn disco "2001" the dance floor is crowded. Then as Nellie Cotto and her partner, Floyd Chisolm, intensify their dance, others notice and drop away to leave the floor for them alone. In that scene, where the multicolored lights flash from above and below and the beat pounds relentlessly on, how many know

47

◄ *The Jacob's Pillow Dancers, a Spanish dance troupe, performs in* The Joy of Bach. *Flamenco dancer Teodoro Morca is at center.*

that the music they are hearing was first created by Johann Sebastian Bach?

"Dance? To complicated, contrapuntal, cerebral old Bach? By all means, dance," says the host, Brian Blessed, in *The Joy of Bach*. "You see, in his day a musician could earn his bread and beer in mainly two places—the church or the court—and between the two, Bach swung." As Blessed reminds us, it was Bach himself who called his music for dance "delights for the spirit."

3

Joy in Portraying Bach

I watched him as he entered historic St. Thomas Church in Leipzig. He had just come from the makeup room in the parish hall. His white wig seemed to fit well. I was relieved. A too-fancy wig would make him appear ludicrous. His costume was also just right. Black frock coat and breeches.

He slipped into a pew. Most others were too busy to notice. The director and the cinematographer were in a huddle over camera angles while the lighting was being arranged. A prop man was placing a little shelf over a light switch to cover it and was putting a candle and a book on the shelf. It was all that was needed to make the setting authentically representative of 1723. We were filming in the transept, the only portion of the old church that had escaped renovation and change; it has remained exactly as it was in the early 18th century—the same arches, the same paintings on the wall, the same wrought-iron gates.

He sat there quietly. He seemed to be in a kind of

trance. Perhaps he was meditating. Perhaps rehearsing his lines silently. He didn't seem to look up when the choir boys came in. They were shepherded by their conductor, the St. Thomas cantor, Professor Hans-Joachim Rotzsch. He had selected a smaller group from his larger choir, the famed Thomanerchor, to be costumed and sing in a scene for *The Joy of Bach* film, recreating a rehearsal as it would have been in Bach's own time. The singers seemed unperturbed by the situation. They calmly divested themselves of 20th century appurtenances (cameras, watches, glasses) as they took their places in front of the camera.

The cantor asked for a rehearsal. They were to sing the opening chorus from the *Christmas Oratorio* from memory, without accompaniment and without scores. He gave them the pitch and the downbeat. Suddenly the huge vaulted church resonated with the heavenly sound of these boy singers. The sopranos pierced the air with *"Jauchzet, frohlocket . . ."* and the marcato tones produced a lively echo.

The bewigged actor looked up from his pew. Almost as if he were magnetized by the music, he walked over to the boys who were singing. Without waiting for instructions from the director, he began moving among the singers. He directed them. He listened to each of the youngsters as he mingled with them. He would frown or smile, depending upon his reaction to a particular voice. He leaned down to give a careful listen to the smallest of the boys. He knew what to do. He belonged here. The script was coming alive. In that moment I knew that actor Brian Blessed was Bach.

All of us in the church seemed to share the same exhilarating awareness that this combination was ideal. Before the actual filming began, Brian Blessed asked Cantor

Rotzsch to check his conducting to make sure it was appropriate. Even though Blessed had studied conducting in London at the Yehudi Menuhin Institute before reporting to Leipzig for the filming, he knew that Professor Rotzsch was in the lineage of Bach himself and no finer coach could be found anywhere.

"It was an overwhelming experience for me," Blessed told me later. "The hair underneath my wig was standing on end! When I had finished that scene directing the St. Thomas choir boys, I was virtually in tears. I had to go and rest in a corner of the church and keep away from everybody."

We had found Brian Blessed in London. Like most fine British actors, he was a veteran of stage, films, television, and radio. He had once done some readings as Martin Luther for a Lutheran-sponsored pageant. He had played Johannes Brahms for the BBC some years ago. Even though we first met him in England we really discovered him in the United States. We were impressed with his powerful performance as Caesar Augustus in the series, "I, Claudius," the Public Broadcasting Service's Masterpiece Theater.

Quite independently, both Lothar Wolff and I came to the same conclusion from watching Blessed in that series. I was impressed by his profile, which struck me as similar to Bach's, according to some of the etchings and paintings I had seen in our research materials. But what really convinced me were the age changes that took place over the weeks in the character of Augustus. It was more than makeup, important as that was. Blessed had an inner projection that convinced the audience that the character really had aged. I wanted our actor for Bach to be convincing both as a young man in his 30s and as a man in his 60s. Meanwhile, Wolff was also watching "I, Clau-

dius" and was similarly impressed. His wife Vee had been the first to say, rather casually, "Wouldn't he make a good Bach?"

We met Blessed in London and he was immediately interested. Although we were clearly convinced that he was our man, we needed to be sure that others would agree. We had often said that choosing the right actor to play the role of Bach could be the single most important decision we would make with this production. And it was not only his appearing in costume as Bach; the same actor had to serve as the host for the program. The idea was that the person who told us about Bach and his music would be the personality who would slip into character as Bach. Not only did he have to look right and act right in front of the camera with a wig on, he had to take his wig off and project directly to the audience through the camera lens.

A screen test was proposed. It was arranged in London at one of the Baroque era mansions of the Public Trust. When our production advisors in New York saw the film, they were convinced that we had found a "blessed" Bach!

"It was really a voyage of discovery for me," Blessed said of his playing the part of Bach. "Through the years I had always been devoted to Sibelius and Stravinsky. Bach was something very new to me. He rather took me by surprise. I think the English people put me off Bach. They tend to talk about Bach the way they talk about Paris. I've been all over the world, I have climbed some of the highest mountains in South America, but I have never been to Paris. Why? Because the English people have put me off. They talk about it as if they own it. And people have often talked about Bach as if they own

53

British actor Brian Blessed, who portrays Bach in The Joy of Bach, *is shown in the Old City Hall of Leipzig, East Germany.*

him. The English tend to do that. But suddenly I've discovered Bach for myself. And he's not at all like that."

How does the man who had to interpret Bach on the screen see this composer? Does getting inside the character give an actor any special insight? "Well, he is an extraordinary man, this Bach," answered Blessed. He continued to speak of the composer in the present tense, almost as someone currently alive. "He seems to be directly connected with God. God seems to pervade his whole life. You feel this connection all the time. For me there is no doubt at all that Bach has this wonderful, deep affinity with God. He has this God-given gift. He is determined to reproduce what he is receiving, and he does this in spite of great odds and even against the establishment.

"It reminds me of Stravinsky. When someone asked him how he had written *The Rite of Spring*, he told them, 'I heard . . . and I wrote what I heard!' I feel that with Bach it is much more so. He's continually under the spell. I'm amazed that he could lead such a family life, to meet friends and have children and be such a successful family man. The actual output of Bach overwhelms me—that he created so much. It's incredible."

Brian Blessed had the unusual assignment and burden of playing two roles in *The Joy of Bach*. What kind of experience was that for an actor? "It was difficult. But it seemed to work itself out. As the host I knew I must not be Bach. There had to be a difference. I like to think of the host as a sort of liaison between Bach's day and our present time. I think my chubby face and maybe my chemistry seems somehow to make this possible. And of course, if that is true, I'm very pleased about it.

"I can be very objective about myself. If I'm lousy, I'm lousy. But my face works with both ages. Obviously the

54

Brian Blessed studies paintings of ►
Bach's contemporaries among the patriarchs
of Leipzig, with whom he had many
disagreements.

host has a tremendous enthusiasm about Bach and a love for the subject. It was really a welcome relief when I could step out of costume, take off my wig, and be me, the host for the program."

We asked him to explain what he meant by "relief." "If you're playing Bach, you are to a certain extent under the jurisdiction of Bach, that is from the work you've done on him. And I might say also under the jurisdiction of God. You see, you really feel quite close to God when you're Bach. And when you're playing the host it seems as if you are allowed to come down to earth a little, allowed to be enthusiastic. Like a child. Really say what you feel about Bach. And it's a kind of welcome relief to do that."

Aside from the composer's spirituality, what kind of fellow did Brian Blessed sense Johann Sebastian Bach to be? "A perfectionist. Oh yes, he is always striving, one feels, for perfection. And he frequently gets on the wrong side of people because of that, you know. They tend to take it personally. He'll complain about the organ with the organ builder, Silbermann, and he'll complain to the Leipzig city councilors about the conditions of his work even though they were really quite good to him. But because he was always after perfection, he was pretty harsh with them. And when his instruments and his singers weren't quite right he tended to be rather abrasive. All of this was because he was such a perfectionist."

Some actors never look at themselves on the screen. They don't want to have their own inner image of themselves in a character role upset by the literal reflection they get from cinematography. But not Brian Blessed. He looked at a "rough cut" of *The Joy of Bach* when he came to New York from London in order to record narration sequences.

"I was enormously moved by it. I've seen myself enough over many years of films and television. I know what my face looks like and I can be very objective about it. And I'm surprised that it fits into the film so well. I find the film very exciting. The story of Bach is told in the film much more than it would be if you had done a film all about his life.

"In the film that we have made there's a great deal of everybody in it. Hundreds of people are in it, dancing, singing, playing instruments. The writer has found just the right blend of Bach and the people of today. There's a tremendous universality in it. We make a transition from the young Bach to the old Bach in the film without anyone really becoming aware of it. And in the film Bach does die. In an ordinary film, that would have been the end. But in *The Joy of Bach*, Bach's story doesn't end. It goes on. A rocket goes into space with his record on board, showing the limitlessness of his music in relation to the limitlessness of his spirit. I find this an absolute stroke of genius."

There are actually only a few moments within the film where Brian Blessed is on the screen in vignettes, recreating scenes from Bach's life. The producers wanted to avoid competing with the music. As an actor, was he disappointed at such a thin script with a limited scope for development and character? "No, quite the reverse. It can be a kind of disease for an actor always to want more and more, and I hope as an actor and as a human being I have avoided that sort of greed. I find that the author has brought about the maximum effect with the minimum of effort. And that is grace. I find it absolutely perfect. I wouldn't want any more. I wouldn't want one speech more."

I thought back to our experience with Brian Blessed in

the German Democratic Republic. There was one particular time when he gave us some anxiety. We were driving from East Berlin to Potsdam to film the scenes depicting Bach's visit to the magnificent palace, to be received and honored by the king, Frederick the Great. We were stopped by the police. They had spotted our West Berlin license plates and this was reason enough to check us out.

We all pulled out our passports. But not Brian. He didn't have his with him. He had left it at the hotel. He didn't realize that in East Germany and in any communist country, unlike in Great Britain or the U. S., all people—citizens and foreigners alike—always carry their passports or identification papers. We had visions of being hauled in to the police headquarters, delaying our filming, and creating an international incident. But fortunately one of our East German television colleagues was traveling ahead of us in another car, and when he no longer saw our car following him, he turned back and came to our rescue. He pulled up with screeching brakes, jumped out of his car, and flashed an identifying card or badge to the police. Almost instantly we were saluted and sent on our way to Potsdam.

Another time in Leipzig, Brian got separated from his luggage. We were checking out of the hotel early in the morning in order to travel on to the next town where we would film, Karl-Marx Stadt. Blessed dropped his suitcase with some others in the lobby on his way into the breakfast room. After eating he returned to find all of the bags, including his, gone. We later found out that it was on its way to Moscow with the baggage of a tour group that had also been in our hotel. Finally, two weeks later, just as we were all leaving the country after our work was done, Brian got his suitcase back. But it had

59

◄ *In his role as the host of* The Joy of Bach, *actor Brian Blessed is able to "step out" of the character of Bach.*

taken intervention by the Soviet embassy in order to accomplish its return in that relatively short time.

What did he think about the experience of filming the Bach story in the country where it happened? "It wouldn't have been the same anywhere else. It was absolutely written that it should be filmed in East Germany. It was a wonderful experience to go into the church in Leipzig and to walk where Bach walked.

"There's a great wall between East and West and it's quite an awful thing to experience going through that wall. It shows the stupidities of mankind more than anything else. But it's another kind of experience to go over there and meet those German artists and the incredibly professional crew. And to work with Regina Werner, the fabulous soprano who played my wife, Anna Magdalena, and did it so deliciously. She told me that we—our team —to a certain extent melted that wall. Something of the wall has disappeared. So, not only were we doing Bach, this wonderful subject with so much power within it, but we were beginning to transcend some of the negative things that exist between East and West. It was a marvelous thing. One felt that one had put one's hand through that wall and shaken hands with people over there. People are the same everywhere."

Many who see *The Joy of Bach* are amazed to see Brian Blessed playing the organ so brilliantly. They wonder how lucky we could be to find an actor who could do that. Actually someone else—a prominent Leipzig organist, Walter Heinz Bernstein—recorded the Toccata in D Minor, although Blessed simulated the playing rather expertly. While not an organist, he is a musician. For over 20 years he has studied singing.

Blessed explained that he had been trained for opera not in order to undertake operatic roles on the stage but rather in order to develop his vocal capacities as a resource for the demands of his acting. He demonstrated how, because of his operatic exercises, he could open up and bellow with full Shakespearean intensity! Of course, all of that musical training was useful in his understanding the man Bach.

"One is never quite the same again once Bach has touched you," Brian concluded. "There's no doubt at all about it. I've grown spiritually myself. Playing Bach has been a very wonderful and disturbing experience. For me it's been a tremendous reawakening. I've really become a student of Bach. I am listening to as much of his music as I possibly can and I'm finding him now, of all the composers, almost limitless. I'm really under a spell.

"One feels one's soul as one feels one's heart. It's a spiritual thing. I will never be quite the same again."

4
Joy and Stress
for a
Court Musician

Johann Sebastian Bach in jail?

Yes. He spent the final month of his employment in Weimar under arrest in the county judge's "place of detention." He was stubborn, the official record says. And the duke he worked for—pious and stuffy Wilhelm Ernst—was stubborn, too. And vindictive. Bach was the loser. He was jailed. The duke was a loser too, even though he had all the power on his side. He lost Bach.

It was 1717. Bach could look back on nine very good years as a court musician in Weimar. The joy in his life came from a good marriage to his cousin, Maria Barbara Bach, and from a fulfilling vocation as a professional musician in a position where he could both perform and compose for an appreciative audience.

But Bach's career at Weimar was not all joy. His arrest indicates there was stress also. His "crime," technically, was insubordination. He wanted to leave Duke Wilhelm Ernst's court and take another position he had been offered. He asked for a release and was refused. The refusal may not have been just because the duke did not want to lose a good musician; it was also probably related to Bach's wanting to cross over to the other side in a family feud.

Bach persisted, and apparently wouldn't take no for an answer. He was in a tough spot. He had already said yes to his new employer and been on his payroll for three months! The new post was at Coethen, as *Capellmeister* or director of music for Prince Leopold, a dashing young ruler who was everything that Duke Wilhelm Ernst was not—and a musician besides.

If the duke of Weimar thought he could use arrest to intimidate Bach into staying in his service, he was mistaken. On the other hand, if he merely wanted to punish Bach before releasing him with a "dishonorable discharge," he underestimated his employee. Bach may have been somewhat uncomfortable under lock and key in the detention quarters, and he may have worried about his wife and their four children, but having all that time on his hands was a gift that he must have welcomed. At last he had time to think musically, to create sounds and write them down. No doubt he asked for pen, ink, and paper with his bread, cheese, sausage, and beer.

Many scholars feel that while in jail Bach worked on the chorale preludes for organ that formed his famous *Orgelbüchlein* ("Little Organ Book") with its double-barreled dedication, "In praise of the Almighty's will and for my neighbor's greater skill." Others feel that he may have begun the epic work, finished later in Coethen, known as *Das Wohl-Temperirte Clavier*, ("Well-Tempered Clavier" [keyboard]) that also had a flowery dedication: "For the use and profit of the musical youth desirous of learning as well as for the pastime of those already skilled in this study."

Bach had concentrated on organ at Weimar. It was

Photo captions for pages 65-72

1   Concert guitarist Christopher Parkening performed near his home in Bozeman, Montana.

2   Members of the Brooklyn Boys' Chorus, directed by James McCarthy, sing "Jesu, Joy of Man's Desiring."

3   Larry Adler performs a number of compositions by J. S. Bach on the mouth organ.

4   Members of the Good Shepherd Lutheran Church Bell Choir in Minneapolis perform *"Wie schön leuchtet."*

5   Brian Blessed is filmed as the host of *The Joy of Bach* on location in Leipzig.

6   British actor Brian Blessed, who portrays Johann Sebastian Bach in the film, also starred in the TV production "I Claudius," on Masterpiece Theater.

7   Bach spent the final month of his employment in Weimar imprisoned by the duke, who feared he might find a job elsewhere.

8   After Bach's first wife, Maria Barbara died, he married Anna Magdalena. A talented musician, she assisted Bach in his work and no doubt performed some of his compositions.

9   Film director Paul Lammers gives instructions to Brian Blessed in a reenacted court scene.

10   While serving in the Coethen court, Bach wrote music for the prince's many social events.

11   Bach conducted the boys' choir at St. Thomas Church in Leipzig.

12   Bach (Brian Blessed) is shown moving among the choir boys at St. Thomas Church, listening to individual voices.

13   Bach was criticized frequently by the city council of Leipzig, and is shown here appearing before them.

14   The Leipzig City Council.

15   Late in his career Bach was honored by an invitation to play for Frederick the Great in Potsdam. He is shown with his son Carl Philipp Emmanuel Bach (Frank Schenk).

16   Bach performs for Frederick the Great.

there that he wrote the bulk of his works for that instrument. His basic assignment now was to be organist at the castle church. The duke was a fervent Lutheran and worship was important to him. The chapel, nicknamed "*Himmelsburg*," was ornate. It had an obelisk-shaped altar and three balconies, and the organ music came from "heaven," a high loft located up under the dome of the structure.

Duke Wilhelm Ernst must truly have been proud to have guests worship with him. He could share with them the fabulous music produced by his organist, who was becoming more and more widely recognized as one of the finest virtuoso organ artists in all Europe. Not only could Bach play the instrument; he was in demand also as a specialist who could test new or rebuilt church organs. If Bach had approved an organ, a church knew it got its money's worth.

Bach was not only the court organist, but was also ultimately given the title concertmaster. Yet the understanding was that he was to be merely a deputy to the deputy music chief for the court, Salomo Drese. Drese was elderly and ill and on the verge of retirement when Bach first came to Weimar, and Bach had every reason to expect that he might succeed him. But the old *Capellmeister's* son, Johann Wilhelm Drese, had been named his father's assistant and was considered the heir apparent. The only problem was that young Drese could not compose very well, and at that time it was expected that the person in charge of the court musicians would create a fresh cantata at least once a month. When after a few years it became clear that Bach could do this and young Drese could not, Bach was promoted. He continued playing the organ but now was also permitted to write and direct the performance of cantatas.

Titled or not, a court musician in those days did not hold a very exalted position. Members of the music staff were considered servants. On state occasions Bach would have to don his uniform or livery. He would not only look like a hired hand, but would be treated like one. Some of the orchestra players could eat at the court, while others received an allowance for food. Bach had a home in Weimar, and in addition to his salary received an allowance for firewood. The elder Drese enjoyed the additional perquisite due a man of his position of one small loaf of bread and one measure of beer from the cellar each day.

Nevertheless, Bach could find a good deal to be thankful for in Weimar. Among his blessings were these:

● He had a staff of competent musicians, both instrumentalists and vocalists, with whom he could collaborate. When he wrote cantatas he knew this group was able to perform them.

● A good friend, distant relative, and fellow musician (Johann Gottfried Walther) was organist in the large town church in Weimar. The two of them had fun testing each other's sight-reading ability.

● He had teaching opportunities: his nephew from Ohrdruf lived with the Bach family in order to study music; Johann Tobias Krebs, who later became a well-known composer, regularly walked many miles to take lessons from both Bach and Walther; and two princes from the royal family were also Bach's pupils, studying composition and keyboard technique.

● He had a librettist to supply his cantata texts. The head librarian at the Weimar castle, Salomon Franck, was also a poet and former law student. He authored a

◀ *Musicians used Baroque instruments and played in a castle that still appears as it did in Bach's time.*

number of Bach's works, including a 1715 Easter cantata (BWV 31). Because he was an expert numismatist, he was also in charge of the duke's coin collection.

Johann Sebastian Bach must have taken special joy in the trips he was permitted to make as an official musician in a ducal court. In his lifetime, though, he really traveled within only a very limited radius—hardly ever more than 100 miles from his home. And the trips that were otherwise joyous or pleasurable were often marred by sorrow.

On February 23, 1713, for example, it is likely that Bach and his orchestra traveled to the castle at Weissenfels, a neighboring dukedom some 35 miles northeast of Weimar on the road to Leipzig. It was the birthday of Duke Christian of Weissenfels and Bach had written his "Hunting Cantata" (BWV 208) for the occasion. It was to be a party for nobility, and the entertainment provided by Bach and his musicians would most likely take place in a hunting lodge.

Bach must have enjoyed what for him would be a rare fling at opera—or the closest to opera or the operatic style that he would get. He used a frivolous libretto based on the mythological characters of Pan, Pales, Diana, and Endymion. The dialog or conversation between the arias was in the recitative style of early opera that was also just beginning to creep into sacred music. Among the arias that premiered that day was the one many recognize today as "Sheep May Safely Graze."

Bach looked forward to seeing his good friend Adam Weltig, a falsetto singer who had earlier transferred to Weissenfels from Weimar, where he and Bach had worked together. But Bach's joy on that occasion, as on so many others in his life, was counterpointed by sorrow. While he was entertaining the nobility at Weissenfels with the "Hunting Cantata" on February 23 (if the latest redating of that work to 1713 is correct), back in Weimar his wife, Maria Barbara, was giving birth to twins—a boy and a girl. The records show that they died the same day they were born.

Seven years later, Bach was on a summer holiday with his next employer, Prince Leopold. They had gone to the famous Carlsbad spa where Leopold carried on socially in the evenings—bringing his own musical retinue—while enjoying the baths by day. It is likely that during one of these holiday trips the Margrave of Brandenburg heard Bach's music and asked him to compose some similar works for his own court near Berlin. The result was the set of six Brandenburg Concerti that today are among Bach's most familiar compositions.

But the heady stimulation of the Carlsbad trip in 1720 was instantly exchanged for tragedy when Bach returned to Coethen. He found that his beloved Maria Barbara had died while he was away. No telegrams, telephone calls, or express mail in those days to inform a man away from home that his children were motherless and he was a widower!

Even before leaving Weimar for Coethen, Bach had an experience in Dresden that must have given him great personal satisfaction. It certainly added to the legend growing all over Europe that he was a brilliant keyboard artist and had no peer. (Only a few persons in those early years appreciated his prowess as a composer.)

In September of 1717 he was invited by the king's concertmaster to come to Dresden. The invitation was eagerly accepted; perhaps Bach thought he might be able to play for the king himself. But apparently what Volumier, the concertmaster, had in mind was to set up a musical contest between Bach and the foremost keyboard artist of France, Louis Marchand, who was also visiting in Dresden. Volumier secretly gave Bach the courtesy of an advance opportunity to hear Marchand rehearse. Bach then wrote a letter offering to perform any challenges on the keyboard that Marchand would propose, and also suggesting that he reciprocate. Marchand accepted. But on the day of the contest, when Bach appeared at the mansion of a leading minister of state (the high society of Dresden was assembled for the event), Marchand did not show up. They waited. Finally word came that he had left early that morning on an express coach. Perhaps the shrewd concertmaster had given Marchand the same courtesy; perhaps after secretly overhearing Bach practice, and realizing that he was no match for the German keyboard artist, he had opted for escape over humiliation!

Bach was a hero in Dresden, and the king offered him the considerable sum of 500 Thalers as a gift tribute. But the servant entrusted to take the money to Bach absconded and he had to be content with the honor alone.

There were happy days again for Bach and his family in Coethen. They left Weimar as quickly as they could in December of 1717, after Bach's release from detention with a "bad conduct" discharge.

Coethen is some 80 miles northeast of Weimar. It had been an independent principality within the Duchy of Anhalt since 1603. Leopold's father had died when the prince was only 10; until he came of age, his mother ruled in his stead. She was Lutheran but the court itself was Reformed (Calvinist) and continued to be so under Leopold. Bach was grateful for the Lutheran influence of the prince's mother. Gräfin Gisela Agnes. She had caused a Lutheran church to be established at Coethen, and with it a Lutheran school where Bach could enroll his children.

Bach's years at Coethen brought him both great joy

and sorrow. The source of his joy was mainly the prince himself. Bach had never before had such appreciative patronage, and never would again. Leopold was a music lover and was himself an amateur musician. He had a good bass voice and apparently played several instruments. During his bachelor days he would "sit in" with Bach's musicians during their evening musicales. That the composer was favorably impressed is shown in a letter he wrote to a friend: "I had a gracious prince, who both loved and knew music, and in his service I intended to spend the rest of my life."

Certainly the attitude of his master motivated Bach to voluminous creativity during the Coethen years (1717-1723). Leopold rewarded him not only with approbation and personal interest in his genius, but also paid him well. Bach had almost the highest salary at the court.

Bach named one of his children Leopold Augustus in November of 1718. The prince and his brother, Prince Augustus Ludwig, were sponsors. The joy was turned to sorrow when the infant died within a year.

For Bach these were the halcyon days of the four orchestral suites, the first of two books of the *Well-Tempered Clavier* (a prelude and fugue in each major and minor key), and concertos and sonatas for a variety of instruments. Very little organ music and virtually no sacred cantatas date from the Coethen period.

Life changed for Bach when his wife, Maria Barbara, died. He was 35, and as a 1720 portrait by the artist J. J. Ihles shows, he was a heavy man with fleshy jowls and a double chin; but he still had vigor and good health, ambition and undiminished creativity. He was a father of four children, and now they needed him more than ever. Catherina Dorothea, the oldest, was eleven when her

mother died, and Wilhelm Friedemann was nine. Carl Philipp Emmanuel was six and Johann Gottfried five.

A year and a half later Bach remarried. Anna Magdalena Wilcken, his bride, was the daughter of a court trumpeter from Weissenfels, whom Bach likely knew as a respected member of the professional music fraternity. Anna herself was a musician, a soprano soloist, and it is certainly possible that she sang in some of Bach's musicales at Coethen, even though her appointment was to a nearby court, Anhalt-Zerbst, where she was soloist.

There was no time for Bach and his bride to have a holiday following their simple church wedding in December of 1721. They were too busy preparing for Prince Leopold's wedding. This was perhaps the biggest social event at the Coethen castle during Bach's years there. There would be guests and a round of parties with dancing and feasting. Bach would be expected to prepare special music.

Among the secular cantatas Bach composed, there is a wedding cantata that was written during Bach's Coethen period. It is not unreasonable to speculate that this happy and buoyant work, *Weichet nur, betrübte Schatten* (BWV 202) was written for Leopold's wedding and that, because it is a solo cantata for soprano, the soloist on that occasion was soprano Anna Magdalena Bach.

Bach left Coethen for Leipzig in 1723 even though (as we know from the letter to his boyhood friend) he had expected to remain in Leopold's service for life. But the happy estate he enjoyed so much from December of 1717 to December of 1721 turned sour in 1722. The problem was with the princess, 19-year-old Friederica Henrietta, Leopold's new wife. She liked frothy and light operatic tunes. She didn't appreciate the kind of music Bach wrote and performed. Bach became increasingly

81

◄ *In Bach's day only one or two couples would normally dance at a court event, while others watched and conversed.*

miserable. He returned to church music. He threw himself with the full fervor of his energy and ambition into the creative opportunities in Leipzig, where he received an appointment as cantor. He was responsible for the music in four churches of the city and had teaching duties at the St. Thomas school, where he conducted the choir.

Even though Bach left court service behind him forever when he moved to Leipzig, he could never completely let go of court life. The attraction was still there years later. Perhaps it was the excitement of it, the pageantry, glamor, and sophistication. He had tasted elegance and refinement; the environment of the court that he had experienced for almost 15 years had shaped him. He would always be nostalgic for the pomp and circumstance of noble living. So from time to time in Leipzig, even while cantor there, he would look for opportunities to reassert his former role as a *Capellmeister*.

The documents preserved from that time clearly indicate that when Bach wanted to claim additional clout in petitions or communications to officials outside of Leipzig he would sign himself as "Actual *Capellmeister* to His Highness the Prince of Anhalt-Coethen." He also placed this on the title page of some of his compositions up to five years after leaving Leopold's court. When the prince died in 1728 Bach ceased using his Coethen affiliation. But he acquired a new title to take its place.

Good old Weissenfels had come to the rescue. Evidently Bach felt that he needed to continue his court credentials. He had friends at Weissenfels—not only Adam Weltig the singer, but also his father-in-law, Johann Caspar Wilcken, the trumpeter—and doubtless his fame was also known by Duke Christian, who would find it advantageous to have so illustrious a musician nominally related to his dukedom.

Bach's tenure in Leipzig was marked by petty disputes with the town council, the university officials, and even the rector at St. Thomas. The record shows that he sought intervention in his favor from no less an authority than King Frederick Augustus, known as Augustus the Strong. Although the seat of his kingdom was in Dresden, he was actually the king of Poland, with a realm embracing the area of Germany that included Leipzig. In the 1720s Bach sent at least three letters to the king in order to get the authorities to pay him a stipend for the music post at the University Church, which he claimed was his by virtue of his cantorship. The royal decision was in the end a compromise—Bach both won and lost, gaining some money but losing the point of principle.

Later in the 1730s Bach continued to seek royal help in his fights with authorities. One of those with whom he had a bitter dispute was Ernesti, the rector of the St. Thomas school. Bach had worked beautifully with Ernesti's predecessor, but experienced great conflict with his new administrative superior. He petitioned the city council repeatedly, and finally went over their heads to the king. The answer that came back was no answer at all. It merely advised the council to work the matter out "as you see fit."

Bach clearly curried royal favor. He worked hard to gain the recognition from the seat of the government in Dresden. He performed in Dresden, but so far as we know not before the royal family. But his organ recital was attended by some of the diplomatic corps, including the Russian ambassador. The recital took place on December 1, 1736, a mere two weeks after his designation as "His Majesty's Composer."

In order to secure the coveted appointment, Bach mapped out a strategy for making sure that the king would be impressed by him. This included musical salutes to the king and the queen whenever they came on official business to Leipzig.

On October 5, 1734 the new king and queen were in Leipzig for the autumn *Messe* or fair. With the help of students from the university, Bach wrote and presented a musical serenade by torchlight outside the hotel where the royal family was staying. The music was Bach's cantata No. 215, *Preise dein Glücke, gesegnetes Sachsen.* A contemporary reported the event with these words:

In the evening at seven a cannon was fired and the whole town illuminated. . . . At about nine in the evening the resident students humbly presented a serenade with trumpets and drums to His Majesty, composed by Mr. Joh. Bach, Capellmeister and Cantor at St. Thomas. Six hundred students carried wax torches, and four counts acted as marshalls, leading the music. . . . When the composition was presented, the four counts were graciously permitted to kiss His Majesty's hand. The King, the Queen, and the Princes did not leave the window but listened to the music with great pleasure as long as it lasted (*Bach and His World,* Viking Press, 1968, p. 96).

The joy of that night was shadowed by the death the following day of Bach's friend, trumpeter Gottfried Reiche —who had so brilliantly executed the shrill trumpet flourishes in the cantata the night before.

Later that same year, when Bach was preparing the first presentation of his famed Christmas Oratorio, he used excerpts from secular cantatas—with different words, of course—that originally had been written for royal tributes and performed on visits by the royal family to Leipzig. For example, the opening movement of the Christmas Oratorio was directly taken from a birthday cantata written the year before in honor of the crown princess.

Meanwhile Bach was working on his campaign to win the designation of royal court composer, which ultimately came in 1736. In 1734 he tried to enhance his chances by sending the king a gift. It was nothing less than the Kyrie and Gloria of the B-Minor Mass. When this part of the overall work was completed in 1733 (the balance was finished five or six years later), the Leipzig cantor presented it to the Dresden court with a cover letter, phrased in the elaborate prose that represented proper protocol of the time:

To your Royal Highness I submit in deepest devotion the present slight labor of that knowledge which I have achieved in *musique,* with the most wholly submissive prayer that Your Highness will look upon it with Most Gracious Eyes, according to Your Highness's World-Famous Clemency and not according to poor *composition;* and thus deign to take me under Your Most Mighty Protection.

For some years and up to the present moment I have had the *Directorium* of the Music in the two principal churches in Leipzig, but have innocently had to suffer one injury or another, and on occasion also a diminution of the fees accruing to me in this office; but these injuries would disappear altogether if Your Royal Highness would grant me the favor of conferring upon me a title of Your Highness's Court Capelle, and would let Your High Command for the issuing of such a document go forth to the proper place. Such a most gracious fulfillment of my most humble prayer will bind me to unending devotion, and I offer myself in most indebted obedience to show at all times, upon Your Royal Highness's Most Gracious Desire, my untiring zeal in the composition of music for the church as well as for the orchestra, and to devote my entire forces to the service of Your Highness, remaining in unceasing fidelity.

Your Royal Highness's most humble and most obedient slave

Johann Sebastian Bach

Dresden, July 27, 1733

(*Bach Reader,* Norton, 1966, pp. 128-129.)

In May of 1747, three years before he died, Bach traveled to Potsdam (near Berlin) to visit his son, Carl Philipp Emmanuel, who was employed as a musician in the orchestra attending Frederick the Great.

Frederick would surely have heard of Johann Sebastian Bach, not only because Philipp was in his service, but also because by that time Bach's musical fame had spread—especially among those who were musically sophisticated. The king was a music buff. He played the flute and the great French flautist, Quantz, lived at his Potsdam palace for some years. He had also commissioned some new keyboard instruments known as *pianoforte* or *Hammerklavier* from Gottfried Silbermann, the same friend of Bach's who built fine organs.

The court of Frederick the Great in Potsdam ranged over three huge palaces. As a patron of the arts and a Francophile, Frederick had sought to emulate in his palaces and gardens some of the splendor of Versailles. We can imagine Bach's pride as he was noticed by Frederick the Great and allowed to show his ability. During his lifetime he did not get much favorable press coverage, but the following week a newspaper in Berlin ran this item:

We hear from Potsdam that last Sunday the famous Capellmeister from Leipzig, Mr. Bach, arrived with the intention of hearing the excellent Royal music at that place. In the evening, at about the time when the regular chamber music in the Royal apartments usually begins, His Majesty was informed that the Capellmeister Bach had arrived at Potsdam and was waiting in His Majesty's antechamber for His Majesty's most gracious permission to listen to the music. His August Self immediately gave orders that Bach be admitted, and went, at his entrance, to the so-called "forte and piano," condescending also to play, in person and without any preparation, a theme to be executed by Capellmeister Bach in a fugue. This was done so happily by the aforementioned Capellmeister that not only His Majesty was pleased to show his satisfaction thereat, but also all those present were seized with astonishment. Mr. Bach has found the subject propounded to him so exceedingly beautiful that he intends to set it down on paper in a regular fugue and have it engraved on copper. On Monday, the famous man was heard on the organ in the Church of the Holy Ghost at Potsdam and earned general acclaim from the auditors attending in great number. In the evening, His Majesty charged him again with the execution of a fugue, in six parts, which he accomplished just as skillfully as on the previous occasion, to the pleasure of His Majesty and to the general admiration (*Bach Reader,* p. 176).

The glory of his reception and honor at the court of Frederick the Great in Potsdam must have been the greatest of Bach's life. But he was 62 years old and his health was deteriorating fast. His eyesight was failing, and he would soon be blind. Bach continued to compose until the very end. He died in 1750 in the midst of dictating to his son-in-law.

Bach was a musical craftsman of his day but he was also a genius. Hans Besch has called him "a citizen in two worlds." He says Bach "knew how to adapt himself to this world, he was acquainted with it, and he could make his way in it. But Bach was a citizen in two worlds. . . . The mood of the baroque personality revolved as in an orbit with two poles: joy of living and death" *(Lutheran Quarterly,* May 1950, pp. 130-131).

Johann Sebastian Bach, the quintessential court composer at the close of the Baroque era, lived with joy and he lived with death.

5

Joy and Tribulation for a Church Musician

The 20-year-old organist was restless. Every Sunday for two years he had been providing music for worship at Arnstadt's New Church. He had been struggling with the town's youth choir; probably because he wasn't much older than the students, he had severe disciplinary problems and complained bitterly about it. The city council complained about him, too.

Young Johann Sebastian Bach wanted some time off. There was so much he wanted to learn about the world of music and there wasn't much outside inspiration available in little Arnstadt. The other two organists in town—both distant relatives of his by marriage—were friendly but not at all in Bach's league. The rector of the school and his son were virtually the only others in the community knowledgeable about music.

Bach wanted to get away for at least a month or so. When he had been a student at the choir school in Lüneburg in his mid-teen years he and his friends had occasionally walked to nearby cultural centers. That meant walking 30 miles to Hamburg, 45 miles to Celle, and 50 miles to Lübeck. The excursions were exciting. They could hear the great organist Adam Reinken in Hamburg and Dietrich Buxtehude in Lübeck, and in Celle they could be exposed to French music performed authentically by French musicians.

Bach chose Lübeck as a place where he might go from Arnstadt to get a quick cultural transfusion. He knew of a cousin who could substitute for him, and he persuaded his superintendent to allow him a leave of four weeks. He stayed away four months! That meant even more trouble with the consistory, of course, but Bach didn't care. He needed the experience.

It was almost the season of Advent when Bach's one-month leave was expiring. If he returned on schedule to Arnstadt he would miss the most famous of Lübeck's musical treats, the traditional *Abendmusiken* or recital evenings that always started the third Sunday in November. Buxtehude would present ambitious choral and orchestral works of sacred music and organ recitals; the congregation in the huge St. Mary's Church *(Marienkirche)* would join in singing psalms and chorales. Bach was easily tempted to stay on beyond his allotted leave.

Buxtehude was nearing retirement and was looking for a successor. Two other fine young musicians had earlier come to Lübeck—Johann Mattheson and Georg Friedrich Händel—and the old organist probably hoped one of them would succeed him. But they retreated. He then became aware of another fine young organist visiting the city. Bach probably wasn't timid in meeting Buxtehude face to face, even though the venerable organist was considered by others to be unapproachable. Doubtless Bach auditioned for Buxtehude and perhaps even studied privately with him. Such an opportunity would have further mandated his remaining in Lübeck rather than returning to Arnstadt, even for Christmas.

If Bach sensed a job opportunity in Lübeck, he would have been foolish at that stage of his career not to promote himself for it or at least to explore carefully the possibility. But there was a catch. It was understood that Buxtehude's successor would have to be a young man who would be prepared to marry the old organist's daughter! Anna Margreta was in her thirties, and Bach was only 20. He was not prepared to pay *that* price, even for what would be a tremendous career advancement.

Besides, there was a young woman back in Arnstadt that Bach was interested in marrying. She was his cousin Maria Barbara Bach. Her grandfather, one of many Bachs who had populated the Arnstadt region for three generations, had earlier been an organist at one of the town's churches for 51 years.

No doubt Johann Sebastian told Maria Barbara all about his experiences in Lübeck. Although it was against the rules, and he was later reprimanded for it, Bach invited her to the organ loft to listen to him practice and demonstrate some of the musical discoveries and insights he had gained in Lübeck.

Bach managed to survive the scolding from the council when he finally reported in, three months late. Even though the records reveal an ongoing official exasperation with the young organist, the suggestion is also there that the councilors had some inkling of the extraordinary talent he represented. One clue to this is that he was paid considerably more than either his predecessors or successors. He was hired in the first place because he had impressed everyone with his organ expertise. He was only 18 when the Arnstadt officials (perhaps at the suggestion of a Bach relative) had summoned him to come from

Weimar, where he had a temporary job as a violinist, to test a new organ. So although the city council was annoyed by his cavalier tardiness, he was not unduly punished for his irresponsibility.

Complaints were registered, however, about his over-ornamented accompaniments for hymn singing during worship. Many were frustrated at not hearing enough of the hymn tune—it was lost in Bach's florid embellishments —and others found the introductions too long. Not surprisingly, Bach overreacted and made the accompaniments too simple and the introductions too short.

In 1707 Bach quit Arnstadt and moved to what he thought might be a better position in the free city of Mühlhausen. The experience was short-lived; he stayed less than a year. Nevertheless Bach's days in Mühlhausen were memorable. Within weeks of starting his new work he returned to Arnstadt to marry Maria Barbara. They were lucky to find a house to live in in Mühlhausen because a devastating fire earlier that year had gutted half the town.

But the main reason Bach retreated quickly from that community was the religious controversy in which he found himself. The church where he played (St. Blasius) was dominated by pietistic Lutherans, and the other church (St. Mary's) was a seat of Lutheran orthodoxy. While Bach apparently avoided personal involvement in any doctrinal conflicts, he found himself uncomfortable among pietists. His theological heritage was more conventionally orthodox. He must have known about the situation before he came, but perhaps he thought that music is music. He apparently learned that pietists favor more sentimental music that is less ornately adorned. While the record indicates no specific problems, Bach

does refer in his resignation to "hindrances" and "vexations."

During the Reformation Mühlhausen had been a center of religious controversy. Thomas Münzer, who had instigated the Saxon peasants to revolt, was captured and executed there. The town had been a center for the Anabaptists, a sect which Luther and other Reformers considered heretical and railed against mercilessly. The lingering religious tension clouded Bach's career and affected the length of his stay there.

For the next 15 years Bach was not, strictly speaking, a church musician. He served nobility rather than a town-church bureaucracy. But even as he left Mühlhausen for the Weimar and Coethen courts, he reiterated in his resignation that his goal continued to be "well-regulated church music to the glory of God." Actually at Weimar he was able to make profound contributions toward achieving that goal through his magnificent organ chorale preludes and his sacred cantatas.

It was in Leipzig, however, that Bach realized most fully his aims of providing the most nearly perfect forms of music for enhancing worship that the world has ever known. And it was in Leipzig that he spent himself in 27 years of intensely creative liturgical labor.

Upon his arrival in Leipzig as cantor in 1723, Bach plunged into a self-assigned task so colossal in scope that we can today only gasp in awe. He had stated years before that he wanted to make possible "well-regulated" church music. Now that he had the chance to direct and organize things for himself in a place where music in worship had a priority, he made the most of it.

Bach observed that the church's worship life had an established plan, an agenda of biblical texts (pericopes) determining in advance the emphasis from Scripture for

93

each Sunday (and other festival days) in a cycle that would not repeat itself for at least three years. The best way to "regulate" music for these worship days, he concluded, was to prepare a different cantata for each Sunday over at least a three-year period, and to base each cantata on the particular biblical text scheduled to be used on the respective day of worship.

Bach not only planned it, he accomplished it. And more. Actually he completed almost five years of weekly cantata compositions, each of them a 20-30 minute work with chorus, orchestra, and soloists. It was a prodigious feat of composition. He not only had to research the texts and chorales as basic resource material, but had to acquire libretti as the basis upon which to build his musical structure.

His literary collaborator was Christian Friedrich Henrici, a local postmaster who did writing as a hobby under the pen name Picander. He was 15 years younger than Bach, and had only limited talents as a poet. But like Bach, he had ambition and was willing to work hard to turn out rapidly, under pressure, the texts that Bach needed to sketch out his interpretive musical ideas. When Picander would use florid prose, Bach would often employ florid musical translations. We don't know whether they worked together as a team, experimenting with this or that idea face to face, or whether Bach would explain what he wanted and let Picander go home to work it out, returning with the finished manuscript. There may have been last-minute emergency sessions to meet a particular deadline. Sometimes, as evidence tells us, their collaboration was a cut-and-paste job. Under pressure—or maybe just because he may have felt it fit perfectly—Bach would "borrow" from himself and interpolate an aria from one cantata or other work into the assignment at hand. We can imagine him saying to Picander, "Here is the aria I want to use again. Please give me a new set of lyrics based on the gospel text for next Sunday."

Writing the music and words for the Sunday cantata was only the beginning. Bach also had to have the parts copied. He enlisted his wife and children to help in this, as well as the students from the choir school at St. Thomas. Then would come the rehearsals.

We can surmise that one of the major frustrations in Bach's life was the painful gap between the heavenly perfection of the sounds he heard in his mind and the imperfection of their human realization by vocalists and instrumentalists he considered inadequate.

After about seven years of struggling with the singers at St. Thomas who failed to measure up to his standards —he didn't blame the boys themselves, he faulted the authorities for not recruiting more able musicians—he wrote a scathing report to the Leipzig City Council, detailing the sad state of musical affairs, and naming names of those he judged musically incorrigible. He also complained to them, "When a musician has to worry about his bread, he cannot think of improving, let alone distinguishing, himself." His point was clear: the only remedy was a more adequate budget.

Bach's task in Leipzig was also complicated by having to arrange for music for all the services in four of the city's churches. In addition to the main church (St. Thomas, where the choir school was located), there was St. Nicholas Church, St. Peter's Church and another one called the New Church. His contract also called for his having responsibility for the music at St. Paul's, the university chapel. For years Bach had had a running dispute with the city fathers about the salary he thought he should be receiving for his responsibilities at St. Paul's but wasn't getting.

At the St. Thomas School Bach was assigned extra duties as a teacher of Latin and as a proctor who had to discipline or curb the youthful excesses of the rambunctious boys at mealtime, bedtime, or wake-up time. Although he had a large family of his own and understood parental supervision, his temperament rebelled at these extra burdens, which siphoned off the energies he wanted to devote to music.

The St. Thomas Church is a landmark of Leipzig. With its sharply pitched roof and round-topped bell tower, it stands imposingly across the main square opposite the old City Hall. It has been there for over 750 years, having been founded as a cloister and hospital in 1212. The great bell has been rung every Sunday for over 500 years. Martin Luther preached in the church on May 25, 1539. Mozart played an organ concert there in 1789, and Wagner was baptized there in 1813. There were 14 cantors before Bach, beginning with the first in 1519 and 15 more following him in direct succession.

For many years the school was in a building annexed to the church. Bach and his family had their apartment in the *Thomasschule*. That meant that they suffered all of the inconveniences of being surrounded by students (including music students who needed to practice) while enjoying some of the benefits of proximity to classes and rehearsals and services.

Bach's cantatas were presented from the rear balcony against the western wall of the long church. The balconies continued up to the transept on both the north and south sides of the church. Today one of the huge stained glass windows along the southern exposure carries the image of Johann Sebastian Bach.

The Joy of Bach *film includes a scene* ▶
with Bach and Gottfried Silbermann, the
famous organ builder (portrayed by
Rolf Hoppe, at left).

In Bach's time there were two organs at St. Thomas. The large one in the rear balcony was old, parts of it dating to the 15th century. Just two years before Bach's arrival it had been completely renovated and rebuilt. The other smaller organ, also old, was up near the front of the church.

With all of his other duties Bach did not normally play for the regular worship services in Leipzig. There were organists assigned to the various churches. Christian Graebner played at St. Thomas until his death in 1729. It is thought that one of his last collaborations with Bach was the first performance of the *St. Matthew Passion* on Good Friday of 1729.

Both the front and the main organs may have been used for that first performance. Bach wrote it for double choir, and in addition there is a smaller third choir that can be used for the chorale theme "O Lamb of God Most Holy" heard in the opening chorus. The documents tell us that in 1736, when the *Passion* was repeated, both organs were used.

The *St. Matthew Passion* was a work that must have given Bach great satisfaction. In 1724 he had composed and presented his *St. John Passion,* which is almost as monumental as the *St. Matthew.* Bach was aware that people in the congregation (and perhaps on the Leipzig town council) thought his music too dramatic, too operatic. Some were uncomfortable with affective music that could penetrate under the skin. Nevertheless he went ahead with even more dramatic intensity in his second setting of the passion story.

Books, articles, and theses have been written expounding on the profundity of the *St. Matthew Passion.* In addition to the narrative continuity provided by the gospel writer (Bach has a tenor soloist "narrate" this in recitative style), there are arias and choruses and chorales that comment, interpret, and react to the biblical drama. While Picander provided some of the words, it was Bach who shaped their communication. Some, like Prof. S. Minear of the Divinity School at Yale University, consider Bach to have been an exegete of the gospel:

Who has expressed more effectively the sense of majesty and mystery which pervades the Matthean narrative? Can there be any doubt that Bach has rightly identified many Matthean motifs. . . . Not only can we say that these motifs are intrinsic to the Matthean narrative, but also that Matthew invited very similar responses from his audience. If Werner Richter was justified in saying that A. Dürer and J. S. Bach have caught the spirit of Luther better than his biographers (as Roland Bainton has reported to me verbally), we can say that Bach has caught the spirit of Matthew better than have many professional exegetes. . . . To be sure, Bach was a musician rather than a historian or theologian, but historians and theologians can learn much from him. Indeed, all of us should thank God for his faithfulness to the Gospel in his vocation as composer. When our own interpretations of Matthew have long been forgotten, his will continue to confront congregations with the crisis and comfort of faith (*Theology Today*, 30 [October, 1973]: 254-255).

There is enough theatricality in the *St. Matthew Passion* for it to be presented as opera. This was done successfully in San Francisco in 1973 with staging by Gerald Freedman and sets designed by Ming Cho Lee. It was repeated in Minneapolis in 1976.

While Bach was preparing the *St. Matthew Passion* he received word that his beloved former patron, Prince Leopold of Coethen, had died. It appears that he felt moved to present a memorial concert for the prince in Coethen. He assembled a group, including several of his own sons who were at the university, and made the trip to Coethen. The music for that occasion was directly borrowed from the *St. Matthew Passion*. He made selections from it and used different words. No doubt that particular music was so much with him during that time that it seemed appropriate to utilize it—even in advance of presenting it at St. Thomas.

One of the treasures within the St. Matthew Passion is the chorale, *O Haupt voll Blut und Wunden* ("O Sacred Head Now Wounded"). Bach harmonized it five different ways within that one work. The melody is virtually the same, but the vertical structure of harmony has subtle distinctions.

Bach did not write many original hymns. Rather his major contribution to hymnody in worship is his arrangement of the great worship songs that came out of the Reformation. Our inheritance from Bach includes 371 different harmonizations of chorales and 69 others for which he provided a "figured bass," a kind of numerical shorthand that allows a trained accompanist to fill in the proper harmony as Bach intended.

The life of Bach reveals that the composer in his later years retreated from the *Sturm und Drang* of the 1720s and 1730s in Leipzig. He no longer produced cantatas week by week. He didn't need to, as he had an ample supply that deserved to be heard over and over. Often he would revise them, inserting new movements or changing their key, or even adding another layer of counterpoint. Borrowing from his own corpus of composition was routine for him, as researcher Norman Carrell has so well established in his book, *Bach the Borrower*. Hardly ever did he appropriate music from other composers, except to arrange and adapt their work (and thus honor them in the process).

No one will ever know how much music Bach actually wrote for the church. So much of it has been lost. Given the circumstances following his death, it is a wonder that we have retained as much as we have. In the first place Bach did not write for the future; he produced music for his own generation. He was not worried about preserving his art. His sons were not concerned about this either. They disposed of their father's personal effects after his death and his accumulated music was often among the items sold. His extant works have been reconstructed in many cases from parts that were copied by members of the family, students, or others. Musicologists are still putting the pieces together, and every now and then a fragment from a concerto or a cantata turns up in some obscure place.

But enough of Bach's monumental creativity remains to provide us with a musical and even theological portrait of the man:

● He was an evangelical Christian. The message was Christocentric. Jesus to him was Lord and Savior, and this was not only acknowledged intellectually but also felt emotionally.

● Sin and forgiveness were emphasized. The devil was real. Bach's religious universe was three-tiered: hell, earth, heaven.

● Death was always close. It was faced forthrightly, and even longed for. Bach's funeral music—motets and *Trauerode* included—is most often bright and upbeat. Paul Foelber has gathered all of the references to death in Bach's cantatas and motets and passions and analyzed them to show, among other things, that Bach used alternate melodic skips of an octave to illustrate the ideas of resurrection and heaven, and that he very often used *pizzicato* (plucking of strings) to suggest the striking of the hour of death (*Bach's Treatment of the Subject of*

Death in His Choral Music, Catholic University of America Press, 1961).

● He was a solid and orthodox Lutheran. He may not have argued or discussed theology except as it related to his musical interpretations, but it is clear in his choral emphases that he understood and followed the confessional (Lutheran) formulas involving sin and grace, redemption, and "justification by faith." At one point he composed a series of organ works based on Luther's catechism. He had theological books in his personal library together with Luther's writings.

One of the reasons why Bach was obscure for almost a century after his death and had to be rediscovered by Felix Mendelssohn and others was that musically and theologically he had gone out of style. His music seemed to cap or complete the Baroque era, and the last years of his life were lived during the upsetting transition to the Rococo period that would lead later to Classicism and Romanticism. Bach's sons were part of the "new wave," of course, and saw their father as an old-fashioned traditionalist.

It was a time of change religiously, as well. After 200 years of living with the Reformation heritage, theologians were beginning to be nudged by rationalism. It is fascinating to realize that the very man who as rector gave Bach such difficulty regarding administrative responsibility for student prefects at the St. Thomas School (or maybe it was the other way around!) became a pioneer in the use of historical criticism of the Bible. He was Johann August Ernesti—15 years younger than Bach, a philologist who felt the written record should be explored as a human document for the sake of a better interpretation of Scripture.

103

◄ *The bell choir of Good Shepherd Lutheran Church in Minneapolis finds one way to perform some of Bach's many contributions to church music.*

Johann Nicolaus Forkel (1749-1818), the earliest of Bach's biographers, and the only one who had the advantage of direct contact and communication with his sons, described the spiritual side of Bach this way:

A man of rigid uprightness, sincerely religious; steeped in his art, earnest and grave, yet not lacking naive humor; ever hospitable and generous, and yet shrewd and cautious; pugnacious when his art was slighted or his rights were infringed; generous in the extreme to his wife and children, and eager to give the latter advantages which he had never known himself; a lover of sound theology, and of piety as deep as it was unpretentious—such were the qualities of one who towers above all other masters of music in moral grandeur (*Johann Sebastian Bach*, Vienna House, 1974, pp. 11-12).

Brian Blessed, the actor who played the role of Bach in the film, *The Joy of Bach* and served as the narrator and host for that presentation, summarized the spiritual dimension of Bach's music:

Above all, it is his music for the church that speaks the essential Bach—not that he drew any distinction between "religious" and "secular." All music was to glorify his Lord. He left us with graphic evidence:

Many manuscripts survive with two curious sets of initials in Bach's hand. At the beginning, "J.J." from the Latin "Jesus help me!" *(Jesu Juva!)* and at the close, "S.D.G." *(Soli Deo Gloria)*—"To the Glory of God Alone."

6

Joy and Sorrow for a Family

He was a Bach. That simple statement spoke volumes. In Germany in the 17th and 18th centuries the word *Bach* really meant "musician." Most of the family hailed from Veit Bach, a miller who was also a zither player. He was the great, great grandfather of Johann Sebastian.

Bach was orphaned when he was 10. He had been born in Eisenach in the shadow of the famous Reformation shrine, the Wartburg—the castle in which Martin Luther was hidden in 1521 after the Diet of Worms and where he translated the Bible into German.

As a town musician his father, Ambrosius Bach, taught him the rudiments of music and violin before he died in 1695, only nine months after the death of the boy's mother. His older brother, Johann Christoph, was now married and had an organist's position in Ohrdruf, 30 miles from Eisenach. Bach was "adopted" by his brother and went to live in his home.

His musical education continued, of course, and now included harpsichord and organ. No doubt the boy who would become the greatest organ virtuoso of Germany and the king of composers established his basic kinship with the king of instruments in Ohrdruf, at the Michaelis Church where his brother played. We can be sure that he explored the organ inside out and practiced as many hours on it as his friends—who must have pumped the air for him—would allow.

Johann Christoph must have been a good teacher. He was surely also a stern taskmaster. The story is told by Bach's first biographer, Forkel, that young Johann Sebastian discovered that his brother had in his music cabinet a special book of compositions by some of the more established composers of that day, such as Pachelbel, Froberger, Böhm, and Buxtehude. He wanted to borrow the book, but for some reason his brother refused. Perhaps Johann Christoph was reserving those pieces for his own study or performances and didn't want the talented youngster in his home to perfect the works first. Johann Sebastian clearly coveted his brother's book, however, and in the middle of the night, when everyone else in the house was asleep, he crept down to sneak the anthology from the cabinet. He took it to his room and began to copy it by moonlight! It took him six months.

According to the story, Johann Christoph found out about it. Perhaps he overheard Johann Sebastian trying out on the organ the music that belonged to him. He promptly impounded the copied volume. (Johann Sebastian did not get the book back until his brother died almost a quarter century later.)

Just a few days before his 15th birthday, as the new century began in 1700, Bach went to school in Lüneburg. His talent had been recognized by that time, of course, and no doubt the Bach family network buzzed with gossip about the young virtuoso living with Johann Christoph. A scholarship was arranged at the choir school of St. Michael's, where he was assured of a classical education while learning music. Bach sang in the boys' choir until his voice changed, after which he became an accompanist. Meanwhile he was studying organ—perhaps with Georg Böhm, organist at St. John's Church in Lüneburg and already a famous organist at age 39. It was *his* music, among others, that he had copied by moonlight! Now he could hear Böhm himself and learn from him.

Bach was never far from family, even when he finished school and had his first full-time job as an organist at Arnstadt. There were Bach cousins in the surrounding area. One of them, Maria Barbara Bach, became his wife.

The wedding was simple and apparently music-less. Later Bach would adorn the nuptial ceremonies of others with his music, but didn't do so for his own wedding. It was held in a small church at Dornheim, a rural hamlet near Arnstadt. By this time Bach was organist in another town, Mühlhausen; his wedding came during a busy fall season, but he returned to the Arnstadt region for his bride. The pastor of the Dornheim church, Lorenz Stauber, was a friend of Bach's (when he had been an 18-year-old organist in his first job at Arnstadt, Stauber had been a theological student there).

About a month before the wedding Bach received a welcome inheritance from an uncle, his mother's brother Tobias Lämmerhirt. It was only 50 guilders, but for Bach the timing was ideal.

Like other families, the Bachs must have had family reunions. We can imagine that when they did come together, they automatically brought musical instruments with them. Certainly there was singing, possibly even dancing. One occasion that may have prompted a reunion of the clan was in 1705 when Johann Sebastian's brother,

Johann Jacob, left to become an oboist in Stockholm. There he played in the army band for King Charles XII. Bach wrote a musical satire for the occasion and entitled it (in Italian) *Capriccio on the Departure of a Beloved Brother*. It includes imitative sounds of the postilion horn announcing the coming and leaving of the coach. It also includes a *quodlibet*, a little musical game where several folk songs are combined and sung simultaneously with harmonious results. Years later Bach also added a *quodlibet* at the end of his *Goldberg Variations*.

The joy of such a family reunion was tempered by the sad realization that Johann Jacob was leaving and his relatives near Arnstadt, Gotha, and Eisenach would probably never see him again.

Johann Sebastian, who had been made fatherless at 10, was himself destined to be the father of a large family. He and his bride, Maria Barbara, remained in their first home only a very short while—less than a year. She was already pregnant when they moved to Weimar, where Bach had an opportunity to be the organist for Duke Wilhelm Ernst and also to play in the court orchestra; ultimately he became the second assistant *Capellmeister*. In Weimar the Bachs had a daughter, Dorothea, and three sons who survived—Wilhelm Friedemann, Carl Philipp Emmanuel, and Gottfried Bernhard. They also had twins who died the day they were born.

It was a given that the Bach children should learn music and become musicians. Several of the sons did become famous in their own right as performers and composers.

As the oldest son, Friedemann was likely favored and given the most rigid instruction by his father. The evidence for this is the *Little Clavier Book for Wilhelm Friedemann Bach,* consisting of preludes, dance tunes,

108

and chorales. One can only imagine the pressure the children of Bach were under as pupils of a perfectionist. They were always in his shadow, and they could not even practice without fear of being overheard and criticized by him.

Bach was innovative in the art of fingering; he decided that there was no longer any valid reason for avoiding the use of the thumb on the harpsichord or organ keyboard. He also spelled out just how he expected his music to be ornamented or embellished by the addition of grace notes corresponding to little squiggle marks—each one a shorthand symbol for extra notes in a rhythmic pattern. His students were expected to finger, if not toe, the mark.

The joy of a happy marriage and a growing talented family was eclipsed in 1720 when Maria Barbara died suddenly. Bach was away from home at the time. We can imagine the drama of his reunion with those motherless children, the oldest of whom was 10. The record does not include the cause of death; there is only a terse announcement in the death register that she was buried on July 7. In those days, however, any number of diseases could suddenly attack and destroy life. She had given birth to seven children.

There are several signs of the depth of sorrow suffered by Bach at the death of his wife. It has been conjectured by Hans Besch that Bach revealed his feelings in one of his most emotional organ works, the Fantasia and Fugue in G Minor.

This work was one of the few organ pieces written during the Coethen period when Bach was concentrating on harpsichord and orchestra works. And yet he took the time to develop in the Fantasia a reflection of inner *Angst* that might be seen as a passionate cry from the human soul for comfort and reassurance. The great fugue that

109

follows the subjective opening movement clearly suggests that the gift of strength, security, and support is being received.

In the months following the death of Maria Barbara there is also evidence that Bach applied for an organist's position in Hamburg. It is thought that one of the pieces he played for his auditors there was the Fantasia and Fugue in G Minor that he had written in Coethen. He wasn't given the post, even though in the opinion of the venerable organist Adam Reinken and a pastor of the church he deserved it. Another organist was given the appointment after he had indicated that he would be willing to make a substantial contribution. Bach may have sought the Hamburg post in order to get a change of location and vocation as a means of assuaging his grief. But there were other opportunities in store for him.

Happily, he was able to marry again soon. One of the few romantic aspects of his life story (in 20th century terms at least!) is his winning the hand of Anna Magdalena Wilcken. Certainly music brought them together. She was a soprano—not just a woman with a pleasant voice, but a professional. She sang at a neighboring court and also made appearances at musical events at Coethen. Anna was the daughter of a professional musician also, a court trumpeter at Weissenfels, named Johann Caspar Wilcken; likely he and Bach had performed together.

Anna Magdalena was only 20 when she and Bach were married in 1721. Her work as a soloist had been at the nearby principality of Anhalt-Zerbst. She had been raised in the town of Zeitz, where her father was lead trumpeter before moving to Duke Christian's court at Weissenfels in 1719. During her teen years Anna may have visited Coethen, and there is an indication that she may have been employed there in the summer and fall of 1721

Bach (Brian Blessed) here gives his ▶
second wife Anna Magdalena Bach (Regina
Werner) a song for her notebook. In the film
she sings "Bist du bei mir."

before their marriage on December 3. The Coethen records show that in September of that year both Johann Sebastian and Anna Magdalena were sponsors at the baptism of a child of the clerk in charge of Prince Leopold's wine cellar.

A strange coincidence linked Bach's second wedding with his first. In 1708, before his marriage to Maria Barbara, he had received an inheritance from his maternal uncle Tobias Lämmerhirt. Thirteen years later, as he approached his second marriage, a second legacy came. This time it was from his late uncle's widow, who died in 1721 and shared her estate with her husband's relatives.

A little insight into Bach's sentimentality has been given us by Anna Magdalena, who saved a little poem that her husband gave her. It was penned on a separate page of her notebook that was a kind of musical scrapbook of his gifts to her, mainly songs and clavier pieces he wanted her to practice:

> I am your servant, bride of mine.
> May you have joy this morning!
> Your wedding gown, your flow'ry crown,
> Your loveliness adorning,
> So fill my heart with love and joy
> That, as this day I meet you,
> My heart and mind together find
> The songs with which to greet you!
> (translation by Elaine E. Lee)

Two years later the family was uprooted again. With his young wife and four children, Bach moved to Leipzig in 1723. Johann Sebastian and Anna Magdalena remained in this Hanseatic city of culture, education, publishing, and trade for the rest of their lives.

The Bach home in Leipzig was situated in an apartment within the St. Thomas School that was attached to the ancient church. The city offered them a number of attractions that had not been available in the other towns in which they had lived: a good school at St. Thomas for the children and a large and famous university. This would be an advantage later for their sons. Cultural and social events would be scheduled. There were also places to relax, like Zimmermann's Coffeehouse. Bach would get the cooperation of musicians among the university students and present secular cantatas in the *al fresco* setting of the coffeehouse gardens.

One of these secular cantatas that reveals some of Bach's humor was his *Coffee Cantata* (BWV 211). If it had been presented at Zimmermann's place it would have had its most appropriate setting. It was a satire on the fad of coffee drinking that was sweeping Europe (it had been introduced to Germany about 1670), and was in reaction to the prohibition against coffee that had been instituted in some places. The lyrics by Bach's collaborator, Picander, seem silly to modern senses, but that is also true of the text material for musical entertainment in general.

We don't know whether Anna Magdalena had the chance to sing professionally in Leipzig or not (she was pregnant much of the time), but the *Coffee Cantata* called for a soprano as well as a baritone, so it is not impossible that Bach enlisted her services. Because she was a woman, she was not allowed to sing for a church service. The question was whether Bach would have thought it appropriate for his wife to sing at the coffeehouse. Most likely he would not have.

Nevertheless, as the *Little Notebook for Anna Magdalena Bach* of 1725 demonstrates, Anna Magdalena did remain interested and active in music to the extent that her domestic and family responsibilities allowed. We do

113

know that she helped her husband by copying parts for his cantatas. Handwriting experts have identified her distinctive notation.

Her collection of music is a lovely anthology of simple songs and tunes that, for all their naive gentleness and technically undemanding quality, are memorable and appear fresh even when they are played over and over. They communicate something of the love, warmth, and *Gemütlichheit* we associate with the Bach household.

Bist du bei mir, one of the songs from Anna's notebook, certainly was sung by her with Bach's accompaniment. We don't know for certain whether he wrote it himself (another name is attached to it in her book) or discovered it and liked it, and so simply wanted her to have it. He may have made an adaptation for her so as to give it his own stamp. Among the 42 items in her collection is also the same aria that Bach later used as the basis for the famous *Goldberg Variations.* There is even a poem about the rambling thoughts of a pipe smoker that may have expressed Bach's own feelings (he may have written it himself but no credit of authorship is given). It has a musical setting in Anna's notebook that appears in two different keys.

Among the Bach legends is the story that he returned home one day to find his older children taunting Gottfried Heinrich, his mentally handicapped son born in 1724. The child had been pounding on the keys of the harpsichord, and the resultant noise was at first laughable and then irritating to the others. Instead of scolding the offending child, Bach reproved the others, explaining that even though they might not appreciate Gottfried Heinrich's musical offering, he was sure that God and the angels found it beautiful!

114

For each of the first 10 years in Leipzig there was either a birth or a death of a child in the Bach family. The total number of children fathered by Johann Sebastian Bach is frequently confused by the fact that so many genealogies did not include female children (at least by name), and also by the fact that when a child died his or her name might be given to one born later. In addition, many of the children had the same first name. Maria Barbara bore seven children and Anna Magdalena bore thirteen.

Bach appeared to enjoy taking his son Friedemann, then a university student, with him to Dresden. There they were able to hear some operas. Leipzig did not yet have access to the same level of opportunity that Dresden had; the latter city was in effect a royal city—King Augustus lived and ruled from there. For Bach and for his son it was a chance to broaden the base of their musical exposure. Forkel reports that the father would say to the son in proposing another opera excursion, "Friedemann, shouldn't we go again to hear the lovely Dresden ditties?"

Bach's third son, Gottfried Bernhard, caused his father considerable grief. He was born in Weimar and was only five when his mother died. He became an organist like his father, and Bach wrote several recommendations for him. At Sangerhausen, where Bernhard had accepted a post, he bungled his financial affairs and then skipped town with debts remaining. The creditors tried to get the young man's father to pay them. Bach wrote in reply in May of 1738:

. . . . I have opened my heart to your Honor, and beg you not to associate me with my son's misconduct, but to accept my assurance that I have done all that a true father, whose children lie very close to his heart, is bound to do to advance their welfare. . . . I respectfully ask your Honor to discover his whereabouts and let me know, in order that, under God's

providence, I may make a last effort to soften his hardened heart and bring him to right senses (*Bach Reader*, pp. 160-161).

Bernhard was apparently missing for the rest of 1738, but he turned up the following January (1739) to matriculate as a law student at the University of Jena. But that career was tragically cut short by his death four months later.

Bach's youngest son, Johann Christian (who was only 15 when Bach died), was the only child who is known to have left the Lutheran church. He became a Roman Catholic, achieving fame as the "English Bach" (sometimes also called the "London Bach"), and living and working both in England and Italy.

Certainly one of the happiest times Bach experienced with his children was near the end of his life when he traveled with his oldest son Friedemann to visit his second son, Carl Philipp Emmanuel, in Potsdam. It was on that trip that Bach was received by Frederick the Great and invited to play for him.

The Potsdam journey by coach with Friedemann would have given the old maestro a good opportunity to reminisce and philosophize in conversation along the way. Friedemann remembered it well, apparently, as it was he who later reported the details of the occasion to a biographer. They went directly to Philipp's quarters, and had hardly settled in when the call came that the king would grant an audience to the *Capellmeister* from Leipzig. Bach was growing more feeble and his eyesight was beginning to fail. But he not only performed with honor before Frederick the Great but also gave an organ recital or demonstration in the Holy Spirit Church of Potsdam the next day.

117

◄ *When Bach played for Frederick the Great, he stood as an unequalled master of the Baroque keyboard. His brilliance as a composer was largely unrecognized.*

Bach's sons surely must have felt proud of their father in that setting. They knew his musical genius. But at the same time they were probably somewhat embarrassed by the old man. He was yesterday's prophet, yesterday's musician. They themselves were in a new age. The Baroque design of things was fading, overshadowed by the Rococo influence that they felt was less florid and more informed by mind and thought. They would create music in the new style. Nevertheless they had their grounding in the rudiments of counterpoint and fugue which would affect all of their creative work. And while their music would evolve to please audiences, it would always seem bland and innocuous when compared with the profundity, depth, and overwhelming power that sprang from their father's creative heart.

A few years before he died, Bach was moved to apply for membership in the Society of Musical Sciences, a prestigious academic organization that survived him by only a quarter century. But at the time it was something he wanted badly enough to allow his portrait to be painted and to write something appropriate in order to qualify. He chose a puzzle canon or *Canon triplex* for six voices. This was printed and sent around in a package to each member of the society. Later it was published in the same musical journal in which Bach's obituary appeared. The canon also appeared on the portrait that the artist Hausmann painted. Bach is shown holding this in his right hand as if offering it to viewers for their inspection.

Bach's blindness has been the subject of considerable conjecture in the modern medical profession. Was the composer's malady chronic glaucoma or did he have cataracts? According to Dr. William B. Ober, associate professor of pathology at New York Medical College,

118

"Hypertensive retinopathy or retinal degeneration in the region of the macula" might have been responsible for Bach's failing vision. He writes:

One has but to glance at Hausmann's portrait of Bach, painted in 1746, when the sitter was sixty-one years old, to recognize that Bach was nearsighted and probably had high blood pressure. The vertical furrows running upward from the bridge of the nose as well as the narrowed eyes indicate Bach's continuous effort to bring distant objects into focus, the result of myopia, or some form of refractive error. The ruddy face, firm jaw, and taut lips hint at hypertension; his choleric, compulsive temperament would match that diagnosis (*New York State Journal of Medicine,* June 15, 1969, pp. 1797-1807).

There has been a debate among Bach scholars as to the religiosity of the composer. For years, because of his intense output of explicitly Christian music firmly grounded in material from Scripture and Lutheran hymnody, it was assumed by everyone that Bach's music was a mirror reflection of his faith. In the early 1960s this was challenged by musicologist Friedrich Blume, after other scholars had revealed that most of Bach's church cantatas were written in the first years at Leipzig rather than scattered throughout his 27 years as the St. Thomas Cantor. But the scholar who did the redating, Alfred Dürr, says he doesn't see how the point of *when* Bach wrote his church cantatas can be used to prove that he was or was not a devout Christian. "I do not see why a man should not be regarded as a church musician and as fully conscious of his bent—just because when he first took office, he devoted superhuman energy to providing himself with a stock of practicable compositions of his own, to be repeated as necessary," Dürr stated. He added, "Indeed I doubt whether it would have been physically

119

possible for Bach to continue such exertions throughout his life" (*Music Times,* 107 [June, 1966]:484-485).

There is a certain dramatic appropriateness in the way Johann Sebastian Bach died. It was 1750. He was now totally blind. He had had an operation on his eyes by the same surgeon who operated on Bach's contemporary (whom he had never met), Georg Friedrich Händel. The operation was a failure. His blindness was a severe handicap, but it did not stop him from continuing to compose.

His final project was the very ambitious *Art of the Fugue.* He could "see" the intermingling of the fugal themes in his mind but could not write them down. For this he depended on the young man in his home who assisted him. This was his son-in-law and pupil, Christoph Altnikol, who was married to Bach's daughter Elizabeth. He must have been a very competent musician to take dictation from Bach. We do not know, of course, whether Bach identified the notes of each voice vertically or horizontally when giving them to Altnikol. More likely he would have played the notes on the harpsichord in a deliberate enough way for the notation to be recorded.

At one point Bach abruptly stopped dictating. He had been involved in an amazing undertaking: creating a fugue with four different subjects, each synchronized into the one work with full development and inversions—the complicated technique of turning the melody of a subject upside down. In his final fugue he had almost worked through three subjects, the third of which was a melody based on the initials of his own name B-A-C-H. (In American terms this would be the equivalent of B flat-A-C-B natural.) It was at that point that he stopped and proposed to Altnikol that he do a choral setting to the music of *When in the Hour of Utmost Need,* but with a dif-

ferent text. The text he chose for his final effort served as
his own most fitting benediction:

Before Thy throne I now appear
O Lord, bow down Thy gracious ear
To me, and cast not from Thy face
Thy sinful child that sues for Grace.

Grant that in peace I close my eyes
But on the last day bid me rise
And let me see Thy face fore'er.
Amen, Amen! Lord, hear my prayer.

Important Dates

in the Life of

J. S. Bach

1685	Birth in Eisenach, March 21
1694	Death of mother
1695	Death of father
1696-1700	Lives with brother in Ohrdruf
1700-1703	Student at Lüneburg choir school
1703	Court violinist at Weimar for six months
1703-1707	Organist at New Church in Arnstadt
1707-1708	Organist at St. Blasius Church in Mühlhausen
1707	Marriage to Maria Barbara Bach, October 17 First published work: Cantata 71 *God is my King*
1708-1717	Organist and court musician at Weimar
1717	Musical challenge to Marchand in Dresden Jailed for one month in Weimar
1717-1723	Music director for Prince Leopold at Coethen
1720	Death of wife, Maria Barbara Audition in Hamburg for organist position

1721	Marriage to Anna Magdalena Wilcke
1723-1750	St. Thomas Cantor in Leipzig
1724	*St. John Passion*, first performance
1729	*St. Matthew Passion*, first performance
1733	B Minor Mass, presentation of Kyrie and Gloria to king
1734-1735	Christmas Oratorio, first performance
1736	Honorary title of Royal Court Composer
1747	Visit to Frederick the Great in Potsdam
1750	Death in Leipzig, July 28

Books About J.S. Bach

Carrell, Norman. *Bach the Borrower*. London: Alen and Unwin, 1967.

Chiapusso, Jan. *Bach's World*. Bloomington: U. of Indiana Press, 1968.

David, H. T. and Mendel, A., eds. *The Bach Reader*. Rev. ed. New York: W. W. Norton & Co., Inc., 1966.

Geiringer, Karl, and Irene. *The Bach Family: Seven Generations of Creative Genius*. New York: Oxford University Press, 1954.

Geiringer, Karl. *Johann Sebastian Bach: The Culmination of an Era*. New York: Oxford University Press, 1966.

Grew, Eva and Sydney. *Bach*. New York: Farrar, Straus, and Giroux, Inc., 1968.

Pirre, Andre. *J. S. Bach*. Trans. by Mervyn Savill from the French Edition of 1907. New York: Orion Press, 1957.

Schweitzer, Albert. *Johann Sebastian Bach*. Trans. from the German edition of 1908 by Ernest Newman (1911); 1st (French) edition 1905. Reprinted, New York: Dover Publications, Inc.; 1966.

Spitta, Philipp. *Johann Sebastian Bach*. Trans. & rev. from the German edition of 1873, 1880 by Clara Bell & J. A. Fuller-Maitland (1883-1885). Reprinted, 3 vols. in 2, New York: Dover Publications, Inc., 1951.

Terry, Charles S. *Bach: A Biography*. Second edition, revised. Oxford and London: Oxford University Press, 1933.

Music of J.S. Bach

Heard in

The Joy of Bach

(title or source, mostly excerpted)	*(performer)*
Goldberg Variations 19	Martha Lovell, Linda Toote and Melanie Feldt, street musicians
Badinerie from Orchestral Suite 2	Swingle Singers
Gavotte from Partita 3 for Unaccompanied Violin	Larry Adler, mouth organ
Gigue from Partita 1 in B Flat	Rosalyn Tureck
Ein' feste Burg (chorale)	Canadian Brass
Allegro from Concerto for Two Harpsichords in C Minor	Collegium Musicum of Paris
Allegro from Brandenburg Concerto 2	Munich Bach Orchestra Karl Richter, conductor
Jesu, Joy of Man's Desiring from Cantata 147	St. Thomas Choir, Leipzig Luther College Nordic Choir Brooklyn Boys Chorus St. Thomas Choir, Leipzig

126

Christmas Oratorio, final chorale	Holy Trinity Lutheran Bach Choir and Orchestra
Wie schön leuchtet (chorale)	Bell Choir, Good Shepherd Lutheran
Gigue from English Suite 3	Michael Jay, synthesizer
Fugue à la Gigue	Virgil Fox with Dave Snyder Revelation Lights
Musette from Anna Magdalena Notebook	Walter Carlos, Moog synthesizer
Gigue from English Suite 3 in G Minor	Rosalyn Tureck, clavichord, harpsichord, piano, and Polymoog
Ich ruf zu dir (Orgelbüchlein)	Erich Piasetski on Silbermann organ
Toccata in D Minor	Walter Bernstein on Silberman organ
Fugue in D Minor	E. Power Biggs, pedal harpsichord
Minuet from Orchestral Suite 4	Baroque court orchestra (reenactment)
Presto from Concerto 5 in F Minor for Harpsichord	Vienna Opera Orchestra, Kurt Redel, conductor
Vivace based on Allegro from Violin Concerto in A Minor	Ekseption, Dutch disco group
"Little" Organ Fugue in G Minor	The Swingle Singers
Jesu, Joy of Man's Desiring (chorale)	Trinidad and Tobago Highlanders Steel Band
Christmas Oratorio (I) opening chorus	St. Thomas Choir and Leipzig Gewandhaus Orchestra
Bist du bei mir	Regina Werner, soprano (reenactment)
Tempo di Bourrée from Partita 1 in B Minor for Unaccompanied Violin	Yehudi Menuhin, violin

Air for the Trumpet	Canadian Brass
Siciliano from Sonata 2 in E Flat for Flute and Harpsichord	Larry Adler, mouth organ with Gary Kessler, guitar
Gavotte from English Suite 6 in D Minor	Andre Benichou, electric guitar and ensemble
Bourrée Anglaise from Sonata in A Minor for Unaccompanied Flute	Jean-Pierre Rampal, flute
Allegro from Violin Concerto 2 in E Major	Karl Suske, violin with Berlin Chamber Orchestra
Sheep May Safely Graze from Cantata 208	Christopher Parkening, guitar
Wir Eilen from Cantata 78	Brooklyn Boys Chorus, James McCarthy, conductor, Gordon Jones, organ
Allegro from Brandenburg Concerto 3	Orchestra of U. S. Marine Band
Fugue from Musical Offering	(reenactment)
St. John Passion, final chorale	St. Thomas Choir and Leipzig Gewandhaus Orchestra, Hans-Joachim Rotsch, conductor
Allegro from Brandenburg Concerto 2	Munich Bach Orchestra, Karl Richter, conductor

Beginning List

of Bach Recordings

There are more recordings of J. S. Bach's music than of any other composer. The Schwann catalog of current releases lists 1016 albums, and this does not include all foreign recordings or those no longer in distribution. The following list is a sampling from among the better-known works of Bach offered without comparative evaluation. An attempt has been made to get a representative grouping of performers. BWV numbers refer to the standard index by Schmieder, who developed the code by which Bach compositions are identified. (3) indicates a three-record set. A number of Bach recordings not available in stores can be obtained through Musical Heritage Society, 14 Park Road, Tinton Falls, N.J. 07724.

Complete Cantatas *(Das Kantatenwerk)* TEL 2635027ff.

This long-term project has already released almost half of the over 200 cantatas of Bach. Nikolaus Harnoncourt and Gustav Leonhardt conduct the performances, many with the Concentus Musicus of Vienna and the Leonhardt Consort. Original instruments are used. Released by Telefunken *(Das Alte Werk)* label.

Other Cantatas

Cantata No. 4   *Christ lag in Todesbanden*
       No. 1   *Wie schön leuchtet der Morgenstern*
                            DG ARC 198465

            Munich Bach Orchestra
            Karl Richter, conductor
            Fischer-Dieskau, soloist

Cantata No. 10   *Meine Seele erhebt den Herrn*
                            LON 26103

            and *Magnificat* BWV 243
            Stuttgart Chamber Orchestra
            Karl Münchinger, conductor
            Ameling, Watts, Krenn, Rintzler, soloists

Cantata No. 51   *Jauchzet Gott in Allen Landen*
       No. 199   *Mein Herze schwimmt im Blut*
                            Phi 6500014

            Deutsche Bach Solisten
            Helmut Winschermann, conductor
            Ameling, soloist

Cantata No. 78   *Jesu, der meine Seele*
                            DG ARC 198197

            and *Magnificat* BWV 243
            Munich Bach Orchestra
            Karl Richter, conductor
            Fischer-Dieskau, soloist

Cantata No. 80   *Ein' feste Burg,* and
       No. 140   *Wachet auf*   DG ARC 198407
            Leipzig Gewandhaus Orchestra
            St. Thomas Church Chorus
            Vaclar Neumann, conductor

Cantata No. 147   *Herz und Mund und Tat und Leben*
                            Ang S 36804

            (includes *Jesu, Joy of Man's Desiring*)
            Motets

King's College Choir
David Willcocks, conductor
Ameling, Baker, Partridge, Shirley-Quirk,
    soloists

Cantata No. 82 *Ich habe genug,* and
    No. 169 *Gott soll allein mein Herze haben*

Ang S 36419

Bath Festival Orchestra
Yehudi Menuhin, conductor
Baker, soloist

Cantata Arias   Sung by Janet Baker   Ang S 37229

Choral Works

Christmas Oratorio   BWV 248 (3)   Ang S 3840

St. Martin's Academy, King's College Choir
Neville Marriner, conductor
Baker, Fischer-Dieskau, soloists

Christmas Oratorio   BWV 248 (3)   DG ARC 2710004

Munich Bach Orchestra
Karl Richter, conductor
Ludwig, Wunderlich, soloists

St. Matthew Passion   BWV 244 (4)   DG 2711012

Berlin Philharmonic
Herbert von Karajan, conductor
Ludwig, Fischer-Dieskau, soloists

St. Matthew Passion   BWV 244 (4)   LON 1431

Stuttgart Chamber Orchestra and
    Boys' Choir
Karl Münchinger, conductor
Pears, Wunderlich, Prey, soloists

St. John Passion   BWV 245 (3)   DG ARC 2710002
Munich Bach Orchestra and Choir
Karl Richter, conductor
Haefliger, Prey, soloists

St. John Passion   BWV 245 (3)   LON 13104
English Chamber Orchestra
Benjamin Britten, conductor
Pears, Shirley-Quirk, soloists

B Minor Mass   BWV 232 (3)   Ang S 3720
New Philharmonic and BBC Chorus
Otto Klemperer, conductor
Baker, Gedda, Prey, soloists

B Minor Mass   BWV 232 (3)   DG 2 709049
Berlin Philharmonic
Herbert von Karajan, conductor
Janowitz, Ludwig, soloists

Motets   BWV 225/30   2 CMS/Oryx 1121/2
Stuttgart Bach Collegium
Helmuth Rilling, conductor

Motets, 2, 4, 6, with Cantata No. 147   Ang S 36804
King's College Choir
David Willcocks, conductor
Ameling, Baker, Shirley-Quirk, soloists

Organ Works

Orgelbüchlein   BWV 599-644, with chorales
Nonesuch HD 73015
Chorus of Gedächtniskirche, Stuttgart
Helmuth Rilling, conductor

Organ Favorites, vol. 2   Col MS 6748
E. Power Biggs, organ

Instrumental Works

Toccata and Fugue in D Minor BWV 565,
Passacaglia and Fugue in A Minor BWV 582,
and Fantasy and Fugue in G Minor BWV 542   Col MS 6804
                    E. Power Biggs, pedal harpsichord

Brandenburg Concerti BWV 1046/51,
plus Orchestral Suites 2/3 (3)   DG 270916
                    Berlin Philharmonic
                    Herbert von Karajan, conductor

Brandenburg Concerti Nos. 2 and 5 BWV 1047/1050,
with Cantata 202 (Wedding)   RCA ARL 1 2788
                    Ravinia Festival Ensemble
                    James Levine, conductor

Brandenburg Concerti BWV 1046/51 (6)   DG ARC 2708013
                    Munich Bach Orchestra
                    Karl Richter, conductor

Suites for Orchestra, BWV 1066/9 (2)   Col M 2 S 755
                    Marlboro Festival Orchestra
                    Pablo Casals, conductor

Suites for Orchestra BWV 1066/9 (2)   Argo ZRG 687/8
                    St. Martin's Academy
                    Neville Marriner, conductor

Sinfonias from Cantatas No. 29, 49, 169, 31
(includes *Jesu, Joy of Man's Desiring*)   Col M-34272
                    Leipzig Gewandhaus Orchestra
                    Hans-Joachim Rotzsch, conductor
                    E. Power Biggs, organ

Sinfonias from Cantatas No. 21, 29, 75, 182, 208,
with Harpsichord Concerto No. 2   CMS/Oryx 68
                    German Bach Soloists
                    Helmut Winschermann, conductor

Concerti (various)   DG ARC 198321

> BWV 1060 for 2 harpsichords
> Munich Bach Orchestra
> Karl Richter, conductor
> Richter and Bilgram
>
> BWV 1043 for 2 violins
> Büchner and Guntner
>
> BWV 1060 for violin & oboe
> Büchner and Shann

Concerti for Harpsichord BWV 1052/1055/1056   Van HM 44

> Vienna State Opera Orchestra
> Miltiadis Caridis, conductor
> Anton Heiller, harpsichord

Sonatas for Flute BWV 1030/1036, 1020, 1038/9,
and Partitas BWV 997, 1013   RCA CRL 3 5820

> Jean-Pierre Rampal
> Robert Veryon-Lacroix
> Jean Huchot

Well-Tempered Clavier, books 1, 2 BWV 846/93 (3)
                                    Col D 3 S 733
                                    Col D 3 M-31525

> Glenn Gould, piano

Well-Tempered Clavier, books 1, 2 BWV 846/93 (2)
                                    Col M 2 32500
                                    Col M 2 32875

> Anthony Newman, harpsichord

Italian Concerto BWV 971,
French Suites BWV 812-17,
English Suites BWV 971,
and Fantasia in C Minor   LON 6748

> Alicia DeLarrocha, piano

134

Partita No. 1 in B Flat,
and No. 2 in C Minor   Ang S 36097
   Igor Kipnis, harpsichord

Goldberg Variations BWV 988   EV 3396
   Rosalyn Tureck, harpsichord

Specialties

Heavy Organ at Carnegie Hall, vol. 1 RCA ARL 1 0081
   Virgil Fox, organ

Ormandy Conducts Bach   RCA ARL 1 1959
   Philadelphia Orchestra
   Eugene Ormandy, conductor

Parkening Plays Bach
(transcriptions of chorale preludes
and fugues for guitar)   Ang S 36041
   Christopher Parkening, guitar

Stokowski Conducts Bach   RCA ARL 1 0880
   London Symphony
   Leopold Stokowski, conductor

Bach's Greatest Hits   PHS 600 097
   Swingle Singers

Bach to Bach   PHS 600 288
   Swingle Singers

Switched-On Bach   Col M S 7194
   Moog Synthesizer

Film Acknowledgments

Cast

Host and Johann Sebastian Bach	Brian Blessed
Anna Magdalena Bach	Regina Werner
Carl Philipp Emmanuel	Frank Schenk
Jailer	Fred Delmare
Silbermann	Rolf Hoppe
Mayor	Max Bernhard
Frederick the Great	Volkmar Kleinert

Staff

Executive Producer	Robert E. A. Lee
Producer	Lothar Wolff
Director	Paul Lammers
Script Writer	Allan Sloane
Editor	Morrie Roizman
Photographers	Ray Christensen
	David DeVries
	Robert Gaffney
	Michel Geller
	Ed Higginson
	Erich Kollmar
	Jacques Nibert
	Wolfgang Pietsch
	Peter Warnecke
	Ronnie Whitehouse
Sound Staff	Wolfgang Donath
	Richard Gramaglia
	Peter Gross
	Werner Laube
	Don Paradise
	Peter Weller
Rerecording Mixer	Peter W. Page
German Democratic Republic Production Staff	Peter Ahrens
	Karl-Heinz Brauer
	Erika Fechner
	Klaus Gendries
	Klaus Gloede
	Werner Kraus
	Gert Moerbitz
	Ruth Mutscher
	Rosemarie Pruse
	Hans Voelker
	Herbert Weigel
German Democratic Republic Music Associates	Walter Heinz Bernstein
	Hans Gruess
	George Mielke
	Manfred Schumann
	Hildegard Zander
Choreographer	Manfred Schnelle

Production Committee	John W. Bachman
	Martin E. Carlson
	William P. Cedfeldt
	Charles DeVries
	Henry Endress
	Richard L. Husfloen
	George S. Schultz
Consultants	Clement W. K. Lee
	James G. Raynor
	Rosalyn Tureck
	Howard Worth
Production Assistants	Allison Caswell
	Carol Zales

Historical sequences filmed on location in the German Democratic Republic at Dessau • Forcheim • Leipzig • Potsdam • Roetha

Record performances courtesy of ABC/Westminster Records • Angel Records • CBS Records • Phonogram Inc. • Polydor Inc. • Deutsche Grammophon

Grateful acknowledgment of grants from The American Lutheran Church • The George Gund Foundation • Lutheran Brotherhood • Lutheran Church in America

Grateful acknowledgment of the cooperation of Bach Archives, Leipzig • The E. Power Biggs Estate • Buena Vista Distribution Company • Centre Georges Pompidou, Paris • DDR Fernsehen • Eton College, England • Good Shepherd Lutheran Church, Brooklyn • Lutheran Church of the Good Shepherd, Minneapolis • National Aeronautics and Space Administration • National Broadcasting Company • St. Augustine Catholic Church, Brooklyn • St. Peter's Church, Manhattan • United Nations